BODY, SPORT AND SOCIETY IN NORDEN

ESSAYS IN CULTURAL HISTORY

BODY, SPORT AND SOCIETY IN NORDEN

ESSAYS IN CULTURAL HISTORY

By *Niels Kayser Nielsen*

AARHUS UNIVERSITY PRESS

Printed in Denmark by Narayana Press, Gylling
ISBN 87 7934 177 2

AARHUS UNIVERSITY PRESS

Langelandsgade 177
DK-8200 Aarhus N
Fax (+45) 89 42 53 80
www.unipress.dk

73 Lime Walk
Headington, Oxford OX3 7AD
Fax (+44) 1865 750 079

Box 511
Oakville, CT 06779
Fax (+1) 860 945 9468

Published with financial support from
Kulturministeriets Udvalg for Idrætsforskning

CONTENTS

ACKNOWLEDGEMENTS

I am pleased to take this opportunity to thank several people who directly, or indirectly, have contributed to the production of this book.

The generous financial support provided by Kulturministeriets Udvalg for Idrætsforskning is much appreciated.

The stimulus for starting the project came in the 1990s with the inspiration of many researchers. These included: In Denmark, my former colleagues at the Institute for Sport and Physical Education at the University of Southern Denmark at Odense; in Finland, Soile Veijola, Esa Sironen and, especially, Henrik Meinander who many years ago invited me to co-edit an anthology on Nordic sport – a joint project which unfortunately never came to fruition for various reasons. Also the good people at the Renvall Institute, Helsinki University: Henrik Stenius and Lars-Folke Landgren. Special thanks to Henrik Stenius, for not only opening academic, but also social, intellectual and even gastronomic doors in Helsinki, Stockholm and Tallinn.

I enjoyed immensely the good discussions with the Gothenburg researchers Lennart K. Persson (Gothenburg University) and Olof Moen (Municiplan). I appreciated very much Olof's academic and practical knowledge in track and field, as well as his research in Swedish stadiums and his congenial arranging of seminars. Lennart's good advice, professorial good humour, and profound knowledge of sport in Sweden – and especially Gothenburg – were also highly appreciated. The same goes without saying for the Nestor of Swedish sports history, Jan Lindroth, who has done so much throughout the years to 'connect' the Nordic sports historians in whose research he has shown a keen interest.

Among Danish historians I am indebted to John T. Lauridsen, Head of the Research Department at the Royal Library in Copenhagen. He has been an ever-encouraging and energetic friend who, on numerous occasions, has been prepared to discuss issues of cultural history with me.

Special thanks to Professor John Bale (University of Keele and University of Aarhus) for being an undying source of knowledge in British as well as Nordic sport, among many other things. I have enjoyed his undogmatic inspiration, congeniality and encouragement during more than 15 years of friendship, and our visits to places like Fønsborg on Funen, Joensuu, Jyväskylä, Exeter, Goodison Park and Anfield Road, not to mention Manchester City's fabulous old stadium on Maine Road. Thanks also to John for invitations to various seminars in both Denmark and the UK.

Aarhus University Press and director Claes Hvidbak deserve thanks for an open-minded attitude to what might have seemed a "one off" project. Thanks also to Mary Lund and Stacey Cozart (Aarhus) and Alan Crozier (Södra Sandby) for their effective translations into English.

Last, but far from least, I wish to thank my wife Brita Engelholm for her support and encouragement over the years. She has not only tolerated my enthusiasm for writing about sport and history, but has also tolerated my frequent absence as a spectator at live football matches in Aarhus and handball matches in Hvide Sande. Finally, I want to thank our two sons, Troels and Thue, for being extremely talented football players as children, and for having stopped playing the game when the time was right!

In acknowledging the help of so many, it must also be said that any errors of fact or judgement are my own.

Niels Kayser Nielsen

Aarhus, May 2005

INTRODUCTION

This book comprises a number of cultural-historical and ethno-graphic studies of the history of sport in Scandinavia. The studies examine the contribution made by sport to the development of Scandinavian nationalism in the nineteenth century, and analyze the ways in which sport became interwoven with the social life of citizens in the various Scandinavian countries in the twentieth century. The main focus of this volume, therefore, is not on the organizational history of sport, nor is it on society vis-á-vis sport – i.e., sport as a reflection of a certain societal constellation. Rather, what is of inter-est is sport in society, and therefore the book aims to illustrate the ways in which sport has been used and has served to help explain and understand Scandinavian society types.

This endeavour is also related to the history of the social classes. In the nineteenth century, while both sport and nationalism were primarily of importance to the bourgeoisie and – in part – the aristocracy, in the twentieth century both sport and nationalism became a matter for wage-earners and salaried employees. It could be expressed as follows: Nationalism – the strongest "ism" of all the political "isms" in both the nineteenth and twentieth centuries – succeeded, through the medium of sport, in reaching all levels of Scandinavian society in the twentieth century. Sport was at the ser-vice of nationalism, but the opposite was also true. Sport also made its own contribution to nationalism: It peacefully and symbolically played a significant role in helping to close the gaps that existed between the social classes in Scandinavia, with working class and peasant being able – through sport – to demonstrate their equality with the other classes in society. In this way, it can be said that sport has also contributed to democratizing the Scandinavian nations.

On the whole, Scandinavian countries were stable and solid societies in the twentieth century. This was, above all, due to the circumstance that they were all characterized by a strong demo-cratic tradition that resulted in part from a sympathetic reform monarchy, and in part from the "association autocracy" that was created in the second half of the nineteenth century. Here people were schooled from childhood in democratic leadership principles, whereby – thanks to the elastic membrane of dialogue and practical problems that had to be solved – much potential dissatisfaction and rebellion were directed into politico-cultural channels, where people had a sense of influence and joint responsibility.

Secondly, in all Scandinavian countries – in both city and countryside – peasants and workers cooperated to a certain extent in forming the so-called "red-soil alliance" (*rød-muldsalliance*). In Denmark, a coalition government existed between the Social Democrats and the Radical Left since 1929, the latter being a consensus-based middle-class party that also represented certain agricultural circles. In Sweden, the Social Democratic Party governed together with the Peasant Party since 1932. In Norway, the same thing happened in 1935, when the Workers' Party sacrificed its traditionally distinctive working-class politics and became a paternal, "nationally responsible" government party. In Finland, the Social Democrats were given a place in the "red-soil" government that Aimo Cajander formed in 1937, a time when the governments were otherwise dominated by academics, peasants and the business community. This consensus form of politics was epitomized by the Swedish concept of *Folkhemmet,* which, with an apparent Scandinavian prototype in P.A. Jensen's textbook from 1863, had been elaborated already around the year 1900 by the socially conservative professor and right-wing politician Rudolf Kjellén, but which in the 1920s was reinterpreted in the direction of a national social democracy. It did not leave much room for radical solutions for either the right or left wing and formed the basis for a nationalism which, as "welfare nationalism", stood in sharp contrast to the fascists' and Nazis' "war nationalism".

Sport and the culture of the body played an essential role in this Scandinavian form of democratic and nationalistic "welfare nationalism", but with regard to sport this support was directed more towards the national aspect than towards democracy as such. It would be hasty, therefore, to credit sports activists – and perhaps even the implementation of the culture of the body in outdoor life – with having played the most important role in democracy. Alone they could not have made this achievement possible, but they did help in the creation of a solid foundation. More important for democracy was the organizational framework of the sports activists. In this respect it must be presumed that the association activities – which also included the sports organizations – and the culture of the body in Scandinavian sports, contributed actively to this – if by nothing else than by weighting equality, mutual dependency and consensus as a form of communication.

Within research into nationalism and democracy a distinction is often made between two paths: a West European and a German-East European path (cf. below). The argument is, first of all, that the Scandinavian trend cannot be unequivocally placed within any of these two spheres. In other words, Scandinavia follows a special path, a *Sonderweg*, that is partly characterized as being a mixture of the two transitional paths. Second, the argument is that the culture of the body and sport play an important role in the Scandinavian trend, in that they contribute to toning Scandinavian political culture in the direction of a certain popular conformity and equality that encourages consensus rather than conflict. However, it is not argued that sports activities and physical experiences have in themselves played any decisive role in the development of Scandinavian democracy. Athletics and sport alone create only silent and mute experiences. These experiences are influential only when they are put into a functional context, i.e. when contextualization takes place in the form of an interplay between economic, social and political factors.

It has been said that democratic populism is the Scandinavian gift to the modern world (Slagstad 2003: 72). This aims at the particular Scandinavian version of democracy as a combination of national statehood and populism – the national being popular, and the popular national. In Scandinavia, the state government has considerable authority and legitimacy, but due to the fact that the distance between state and society is narrower than in so many other places in the world, the tolerance of state interference in the civil life of its citizens is greater in Scandinavia than, for instance, in Germany and France, and also in the UK and Italy, which are traditionally less accustomed to this. Not only is there a difference between Scandinavia and Western Europe, but a difference also presents itself in respect to Eastern Europe: A situation such as that which took place in Poland from 1980-83, when Solidarnosc became a political power factor as a result of the illegitimacy of the state and the sense of an insurmountable threshold between state and society, would never happen in Scandinavian countries (Törnquist

Plewa 1992). Here the state is characterized as being both a home, where the patriarchs take care of their citizens, and an authority that determines and guarantees the rights of its citizens; in other words, the state comprises both emotions and reason in establishing what is right and wrong (Østerberg 1997: 248). It is difficult to conceive of the history of Scandinavia without Hegel.

As part of this hybridization of state and civil society the idea of state-supported general education has played an important role. It has involved steadily increasing popular access to the cultural and political capital of the traditional ruling classes, as well as the popularization of highbrow culture. The sizeable coalition between the bourgeoisie and peasants in the second half of the nineteenth century was followed by a later and larger coalition in the first half of the twentieth century, namely, cooperation between peasants and workers in the precarious 1930s, when the romantic-expressive nationalism of peasant culture was united with the national folk socialism of the working class. By virtue of this hybridization between *Gemeinschaft* and *Gesellschaft,* between tradition and modernity, and between country and city, the right-wing forces in the political landscape had difficulty getting a word in edgeways. Culturally speaking, the space was already occupied, and the social demands that fascism could assert were advanced in Scandinavia by the social-democratic workers' movement, which from the mid-1930s had become a popular movement. All this resembles a clever political master plan that appealed to citizens and not obedient subjects (Slagstad 2003: 77).

But a movement has taken place not only from above and downwards, but also from below and upwards, where particularly sport and the culture of the body have played a role. The special status that popular culture has in Scandinavia as opposed to the rest of Western Europe is linked to this (Kayser Nielsen 2003). Contrary to the situation in Germany and England, football, for instance, has never been a distinctly working-class phenomenon in Scandinavia, but a popular-national sport that not only includes the bottom but also the top – and, above all, the population at large. Likewise, the gymnastics that the Danish peasants introduced as their own at the end of the nineteenth century have since been elevated to a sport for the entire country. Similarly, skiing – that in the first decades of the twentieth century was merely a parade exercise for loggers from the periphery of Norway, Sweden and Finland – is now a national icon. Just think of Vasaloppet, Holmenkollen, and the scandalous abuse of doping in Finnish skiing that tugged at the heartstrings of the Finnish nation.

One of the reasons for this is that sports organizations, and therefore also clubs and associations, have benefited from state support (Kayser Nielsen 1989). Sport – the noblest arena for the cultural development of the lower classes on a mass level – was both a civil and a state forum – i.e., an actual national enterprise. Here one could, as part of the desire for "perfection" so central to Scandinavian educators (Slagstad 1998: 79 f.), endeavour to mould both soul and body.

One of the main objectives of the book is thus to illuminate the relationship between *sport and nationalism*, and in particular to show the role performed by sport in Scandinavian nationalism: both the patriotic nationalism of the nineteenth century and the democratic, welfare-based nationalism constructed in conflict with fascistic forces in all the Scandinavian countries during the interwar period. The other main objective is to bring into focus *differences and similarities between the Scandinavian countries*. Scandinavia is often considered a unity, but upon closer examination considerable differences become apparent. Yet, just as often, when these differences have been elucidated, one can observe the common character and sense of community that does exist.

At least this is my experience. I lived in Sweden for a number of years in the 1970s, and found it most agreeable. There was more space than in Denmark, which at the time was dominated by a poor domestic political climate. The social debates were fiercer in Sweden, even though Denmark understood capital logic better and had closer connections to the fertile German cultural criticism. For several periods in the 1990s I worked as a visiting professor and supervisor at the University of Helsingfors. I felt very much at home and became so familiar with the city of Helsingfors that today I consider it "my" capital more than Copenhagen. Furthermore, from around 1975 until 1995 my family and I spent every single summer holiday in the Finnish skerries, my wife being Fenno-Swedish (we met each other on the Icelandic volcanoes).

These experiences have resulted in my intimate connection with both Scandinavian everyday life and Scandinavian cultural history. I am captivated by Scandinavia's special combination of magical light summertime nights and friendly wintertime darkness, as well as the collective Scandinavian mentality with its special mixture of melancholy, guilt, cultivation of consensus, and obstinate independence. And as a result of my Scandinavian contacts I have seen plenty of sport throughout Scandinavia. It all started in the summer of 1968, when I was an upper secondary school pupil and received a scholarship to attend school in Sweden, where I saw my first Swedish football match. This took place in the late summer in Uddevalla. This was followed by a trip to Reykjavik in 1972, where I saw Allan Simonsen's debut against Iceland. Later I went to the ice hockey rinks in Umeå ("heja Löven") and Vasa, Finland on numerous occasions in the 1970s, as well as in Helsingfors in the 1990s. In the 1980s, I visited Göteborg and especially GAIS, whose website – the best in Scandinavia – I continue to visit. And of course I should not ignore my sports experiences in Denmark, with AGF and Aarhus Stadium at the top of the list. Old love dies hard.

For these reasons – which primarily concern silent, bodily knowledge – I wanted to write a book about sport in Scandinavia in a comparative light; a book that should, at the same time, communicate the fact that sport is at issue, rather than literature or architecture, for instance.

This book is neither purely chronological nor purely thematic in structure, and so its individual parts can be read separately. The short chapter on the 1912 Stockholm Olympics is the pivotal point as far as the subject matter is concerned, and is a good place to start if one does not intend to read the book from cover to cover. The book has four sections: the first one focuses on the state, nation and education in the eighteenth and nineteenth centuries; the second concerns the new bodily awareness that manifested itself from 1900 to 1914; the third is dedicated to the interwar period, and finally the book deals with the political significance of the body, the way in which sports halls contributed to sociality, and the special consensus thinking and conformity that, for better or worse, are Scandinavian hallmarks.

BODY AND ENLIGHTENMENT IN LATE 18TH CENTURY DENMARK

In the summer of 1787 a young official from the Board of Trade, Mathias Lunding, undertook a three-month journey around the Kingdom of Denmark and the Duchies of Slesvig and Holstein to observe the state of industry and domestic crafts in different parts of the country. The idea was his own and it was backed by the Board of Trade which gave him instructions to guide him on his way. The itinerary advised the young lawyer not only to make observations on agriculture but also to visit places in Denmark where "factories of enterprise" were particularly successful. These included glove production in Randers, the machine bleachery in Haderslev, stocking knitting in Hammerum Herred, lace manufacture in Møgeltønder and Tønder, and the new factory in Fredericia. Top priority, however, was given to the domestic linen manufacture with its associated spinning schools in the Næstved district and southern Fyn. It was said, for instance, of the factory in the Barony of Brahetrolleborg that:

> It deserves attention on account of the plan and order that is found there in every class of work and the success the plant has had as regards the many spinning schools that keep up the work without any extraordinary support. (Paludan 1979: 12)

A couple of days after Midsummer 1787, Matthias Lunding set off on his tour. The idea was that he would write a report on his observations so that they could serve as a basis for starting further production operations. The report came to nothing, however, but by good luck Lunding kept a private journal of his travels, which besides giving data on technical and economic matters also contains a wealth of information that is interesting for the history of culture and consciousness. His diary from the journey was published in 1979 in C. Paludan (ed.): "Matthias Lundings rejsedagbog 1787", *Kulturminder* 3. rk, bd. 2. We learn a great deal, not just about what contemporary reality was like, but also how it was perceived, i.e. what a young, ambitious official thought that it was like, or what it ought to be like. As a relic of the age of reason in the late eighteenth century, Lunding's journal is of great value. It is characterized throughout by optimism, enthusiasm about progress, and a zeal for reform, but it also leaves us in no doubt that considerable change was necessary, and that a great deal of work remained to be done. He said of the town of Odense, for example:

> As regards beauty and splendour the town is improving, but it is declining in wealth, and is rather well provided with beggars, especially children. (Paludan 1979: 23)

We notice the tone immediately: the sober bourgeois official's criticism of empty show and shabby genteelness, against the background of his basic pragmatism which also causes him to be alert to idleness and poverty. We can likewise suspect that he sees a certain connection between the lack of production and the begging.

Sensual enlightenment

Six months after Matthias Lunding began his tour, Denmark was visited by another enlightened traveller, the French-Venezuelan revolutionary general and politician Francisco de Miranda, who was educating himself and escaping at the same time by touring Europe. He stayed in Denmark from Christmas 1787 until Easter 1788. He too kept a diary of his observations. Miranda's diary was published in a Danish translation in 1987, commented and edited by H. Rostrup, entitled *Miranda i Danmark. Francisco de Mirandas danske rejsedagbog 1787-1788*. It is instructive to compare it with Lunding's, because they were both moving to some extent in the same reform-minded circles of the nobility and the bourgeoisie. Yet we notice a clear difference in their basic outlook and temperament. Whereas Lunding is subdued and discrete, Miranda is lively and direct. If Lunding is the sober, almost plodding observer, Miranda is the enthusiastic, indignant, and emotional champion of the new ideas. Whereas we have to examine Lunding closely to detect whether he may have visited a brothel in Hamburg while on his travels, Miranda is much more forthright in his description of the Jewish girls who were provided for his nocturnal amusement:

When we had eaten I went to visit my girl, with whom I drank tea, and then I went to bed with her until 11 o'clock, and I screwed her twice. (Rostrup 1987: 75)

Miranda wrote this after first having described a pleasant dinner party the same evening in the English Club, where many of the leading cultural figures and politicians of the day were present. After satisfying his bodily needs, he went home and read Jean-Jacques Rousseau's work on the Polish constitution.

It is clear in general that Miranda is a sensual man with an eye for female beauty, and that he enjoyed life in Copenhagen. He says, for instance, about Ernst Schimmelmann, the minister of finance, that he is young and "married to a likewise young woman who is not bad" (Rostrup 1987: 55). He is referring to Countess Charlotte Schimmelmann. He visits the Schimmelmann family on Christmas Day, drinks tea with them, and talks about literature. For Miranda it was not far from mind to body, but it would be wrong to perceive him as either a pre-modern "nature person" or as a timeless hedonist and skirt-chaser. He is a representative of a personality type at the transition to modernity, for whom the body was entitled to all its rights, but with style: first he drank tea …

He took a keen interest in contemporary political and social matters, which led him to visit the prisons of Copenhagen. Here we see the enlightened citizen of the world, showing his humanistic and philanthropic horror at the dreadful conditions, but also the modern rationalist who, almost like a prototype of Foucault, cannot understand why the prisoners primarily have to suffer punishment to their bodies, with torture and whipping, when they could instead be making themselves useful by doing productive work while they are incarcerated. He thus combined utility with humanism. The same complaint about wasted talent is evident from his description of one of the girls in the House of Correction at Christianshavn:

I saw here a beautiful and strong girl of 18, with the most sensual looks I have ever seen, wild to get screwed – and sentenced to stay here for life! Because she had a child that she was thought to have killed! (Rostrup 1987: 109 ff.)

This is not just an epicurean speaking, but also a pragmatist and an advocate of natural law. Miranda appears to think that nature's gifts should not be allowed to perish unused, but should be fulfilled. For him the human body is not primarily a static lump that is liable to degradation and castigation, but a productive entity which should – albeit preferably with discipline and honour – be allowed to act and develop, whether it be in work or sex. With a patriarchal concern that is typical of the times, he also turned to Ernst Schimmelmann to obtain more humane and rational treatment of prisoners.

In both the slightly cool Lunding and the sensual, passionate Miranda, we thus find that the modern viewpoint, that people, including the weakest members of society, should not so much be punished as improved and disciplined. We likewise note a patriarchal will to intervene and put things right on the basis of the view that activity is better than idleness. The starting point for one of them is of course an economically coloured mercantilism, for the other a sentimental and idealistically coloured libertarian humanism, but the basic attitude is the same: the combination of new rationalistic thought and humane concern, besides a patriarchal know-all attitude. One can also detect a modern understanding that the human body thrives best in activity and vigour. Lunding wrote of his visit to the Vajsen House in Altona that the boys there were healthier and fitter than the girls, "no doubt because they had more movement and freedom"(Paludan 1979: 59 ff.).

At the same time, both men stress the beneficial effects of order and cleanliness, fixed routines and supervision. It is keeping with this that Miranda's attempt to improve prison conditions led to a royal ordinance of 19 May 1798, which ruled that prisoners who had committed serious crimes should be separated from those who were guilty of minor offences and could therefore be improved provided the bodies were properly distributed in time and space. The modern tendency towards parcelling and division is clear enough, along with the emphasis on ordered conditions for matters large and small, ranging from the finances of the realm to children's homes and poor relief. This universalistic tendency and longing for order in the midst of diversity is, despite all the differences in the individual contributions, a recurrent characteristic of the enlightenment project of rationalism. It is primarily general principles that determine both Miranda's reforms and Lunding's observations and descriptions.

Whereas Miranda subsequently disappeared from Danish history, Matthias Lunding continued his work, and in 1789 he succeeded his father as director of the Royal Orphanage for Newborn Children, in keeping with the ideas about the relationship between production, growth, work discipline, and the eradication of poverty which his father's colleague Niels Ryberg had launched in the 1770s. Let us follow Lunding on his trip to spinneries and spinning schools in south Fyn and elsewhere: For epoch-making things were happening in terms of the history of the body, precisely at the time when Lunding started his tour.

In a letter dated 2 July 1787, Sybille Reventlow writes about her husband Johan Ludvig (cf. below):

In the afternoon Ludvig danced with the peasants' children and had them perform a great many physical exercises, and in the evening we all danced with our people. (Reventlow 1902: 114)

This was not a matter of wild, spontaneous play, but staged play, organized and controlled from above. These seem to be the first organized athletic events in Denmark. This was the decisive point: that not only the head but also the body now became an object for enlightenment, education, and imprinting. Even the breaks at the estate schools, when the children had formerly frolicked freely, were now to be brought into organized play.

It is clear from the same letter that Reventlow was busy in those days with the agrarian reforms on his lands, by which the common fields and villages were split up and enclosed in individual lots and farmsteads. On the preceding Sunday he had preached a fiery sermon to his peasants, with such enthusiasm and emotion that his listeners – who included the poet Jens Baggesen – had been moved to tears. We even read that Baggesen wept so violently that he was not himself for the rest of the day.

The question that now forces itself upon us is: what is the connection between these two champions of enlightenment, between Reventlow's agricultural projects and dances with the children, and Baggesen's being moved to tears? Let us look for an answer to this by peering over Lunding's shoulder in south Fyn, and we will see that the events outlined here were not just chance happenings but important occasions in (bodily) history.

In the enlightened districts of southern Fyn

At one of the bends around the castle of Brahetrolleborg there is a monument by the roadside, just before the ascent to the Alps of Fyn, with the inscription "Friend to the Children and Friend to the Peasants". It was raised in memory of the philanthropist, educationalist, politician, and estate owner Johan Ludvig Reventlow. From his seat at Brahetrolleborg he influenced this area of south Fyn in various respects, in a way that is typical of the work of enlightenment and modernization that took place in Denmark in the years leading up to 1800. The obelisk, with a medallion portrait of J.L. Reventlow on the front, was raised in 1888, as we learn from an inscription on the back, to mark the centennial of the abolition of adscription, the law that had tied peasants to the soil, and in memory of the schools founded by Reventlow in the area. Naturally, Matthias Lunding did not see this monument on his journey, but there were other visible signs of the enterprising work of enlightenment and reform. In the desolate area south of the lake Brændegård Sø, in a trial forestry plantation at Bremerhus, we can still see the huge oak trees that J.L. Reventlow – probably in the autumn of 1784 – had planted for use in shipbuilding. The Brahetrolleborg forestry district was in general one of the first places to introduce an organized form of management, as one can confirm for oneself by looking at the solitary estate landscape, devoid of people, between the castle and the Fåborg–Svendborg road.

In the nearby village Gerup, there still stands one of the peasant schools that Reventlow built to promote popular enlightenment on his estate. It originally bore the name Sybillesminde in memory of Reventlow's wife (a sister of Schimmelmann's wife, whom Miranda the charmer found rather pleasing). The Reventlows were close friends of the poet Jens Baggesen, and the district around Brahetrolleborg is full of sites christened by Sybille Reventlow and Jens Baggesen on their emotional strolls in the district. Names like Korinth, Amsterdam, Troja, and Neapel (i.e. Troy and Naples) are the result of the imaginative friends' exalted walks. The more rationalistic side of the enlightenment project can be found in farm names such as Flids-ager ("diligence field") and Nøjsomhedsglæde ("joy of contentment with one's lot"), which bear witness to the virtues extolled by the bourgeoisie in those days.

The poem *Landforvandlingen* (The Transformation of the Land), "written in a hollow oak in the forest at Christianssæde" and with an indirect mention of J.L. Reventlow, depicts in a dreamlike vision the harmonious consequences the agrarian reforms would have for the landscape and the population:

> *Solemn forests, relieved by gentle dales,*
> *Then by limpid rivers as I passed;*
> *All was full of life, by order ruled,*
> *Nature here was intertwined with art;*
> *Scattered lay the happy little roofs,*
> *Under which the earth's great riches lay,*
> *Thither went the man, and here his wife,*
> *He to tend his fields, and she to tend her children.*
> (Baggesen 1907: 300 f.)

We can easily suspect that the staged emotionality – the sentimentalism – and the bold utilitarianism are two sides of the same modernistic enlightenment project. As we shall see below, this dual vision also concerned the attitude to the body, which was now both stylized and sentimentalized.

Here the body is neither an object for rational educational projects as in the young Mathias Lunding, nor a means to a sensual-revolutionary hedonism as in Miranda. Here it is instead an occasion for emotionality. The body is used as a way to alter emotional states; in itself it is of little significance.

J.L. Reventlow was not the only pioneer as regards agrarian reforms and public education in south Fyn. In 1784 the county of Muckadell was created by the amalgamation of four estates, Arreskov, Brobygård, Gelskov, and Ølstedgård. Here Count Schaffalitzky de Muckadell at Arreskov had set up domestic industries, with spinneries and spinning schools for the poor people on the estate, and there was close cooperation with the master linen weaver, I. Chr. Thorning at Brahetrolleborg. The patriarchal and philanthropic element here was expressed in the free issue of medicine to everyone on the estate who needed it. (Paludan 1979: 20).

On the Hvidkilde estate Baron Poul Abraham Lehn, one of the richest landowners in Fyn, who in 1731 had inherited the estate from his uncle Johan Lehn, set up a small cotton factory to produce fustian and ticking. It was managed by Anton Sturm, whose father had emigrated from Germany. Here the poorest of the peasants were taught how to card and spin cotton. It was very important to the baron that this factory, and a comparable one that he owned in Smørum, should not be subsidized by the state factory fund but should survive on its own profits, in the private, liberal spirit (Paludan 1979: 19).

Baron Lehn likewise invested in the improvement of the peasants' farms and housing conditions, and he was generally interested in the well-being of his subjects. He also acted to have the copyholders' farms enclosed and moved out of the villages, just as he was a pioneer and advocate of a series of agrarian reforms. Although he did not show the same airy, romantic zeal as Reventlow, his tenants were among the most prosperous peasants in Fyn, and it was he who laid the foundation for the flourishing fruit-growing and production of fruit wines around Svendborg, by giving his peasants fruit trees. The "alertness" that was to characterize south Fyn in the nineteenth century was due not least to Baron Lehn's many rationalistic initiatives, which provided the basis for material prosperity, which in turn generated a surplus for more spiritual pursuits, the fruits of which were harvested by high schools and free schools throughout the nineteenth and twentieth centuries.

Further west, in Dreslette, we see yet another side of the rationalistic spirit of the age, with reforms and modernization as the guiding stars. In 1785/86 the Councillor and estate owner Niels Ryberg of Hagenskov had an astronomical observatory built here on a platform above the church tower (Rasch 1964: 299). Although the idea was scarcely unchristian, this addition to the church is a visible proof of the rationalistic thirst for change and disregard of the traditions and conceptions of the old world, which meant that even the church and religion were no longer sacrosanct. What was given was no longer

good enough, it had to be expanded and changed. Knowledge, enlightenment, and reforms were the ideals of the times. Enterprise,
growth, and improvement, propelled by bourgeois virtues such as
diligence, thrift, common sense, and a comprehensive outlook were
key words in the minds of these reformers. Niels Ryberg's observatory on Dreslette church is one visible expression of this. At Kong
between Næstved and Vordingborg in Southern Sjælland there is
another. Here Ryberg built a rural factory on his estate of Øbjerg-
gård, and although it, like the other factories, never produced a
surplus, it did lead to a vigorous population growth on the estate in
the first twenty years, and this alone was a sign of success, growth,
and enterprising spirit.

The real purpose may not in any case have been profit, but rather
a demonstration of economic enterprise and patriotic concern for the
population. Also attached to the linen factory in Kong were spinning
schools for the poorest elements of the peasantry, who were to be
taught how to cope for themselves and thus benefit the country.

The awareness of this patriotic belief in helping people to help
themselves is clearly expressed by Lunding, who praises "our patriotic Ryberg" and adds:

So much money has been distributed among the poor in these times
when everything is expensive, and so many young people of both
sexes have thereby been rendered capable of earning their bread and
been prevailed upon to spread this useful branch of manufacturing
enterprise! (Paludan 1979: 77)

The means for this were to be a combination of work and schooling;
people were generally taught for a few hours in the morning and
worked the rest of the time. To support the learning of order, diligence, and discipline in these spinning schools, a number of spinning
songs were written at Rydberg's expense, professing moral virtues.
The author was a clergyman from Ærøskøbing, Hans Chr. Bunkeflod, who in 1783 published *Forsøg til Viser for Spindeskolerne i Sielland*
(An Attempt at Songs for the Spinning Schools of Sjælland). These
versified disciplining tools were used not only in spinning schools
but also in the schools of the Næstved Patriotic Society.

They hit out especially against laziness and drunkenness, enjoining people to obedience and fidelity in general and to employers in particular. They attacked begging and praised industrious work as a way to eliminate it:

> *So many men a-begging go*
> *From house to house, 'tis pity*
> *They suffer and are turned away*
> *Because they could learn nothing*
> *O girls, if they could spin like us*
> *Then they would not go hungry*
> *They would not tread the trackless ground*
> *But they would praise our maker.*
> (Bunkeflod 1786: 12 f.)

And mere spinning was not enough. The employees also had to compete among themselves to see who could spin the most. A song about the bliss of country life says:

> *We all sit here spinning*
> *To see who is winning*
> *Spin well and spin better than me!*
> *I'll wager a treasure*
> *There's no greater pleasure*
> *Than spinning as nicely as we.*
> (Bunkeflod 1786: 8)

These ideals were accompanied by moralizing and admonitory texts in the same spirit, preaching a pragmatic utilitarian morality for all aspects of life, from work to marriage and love. V. K. Hjort's *Sange for unge Piger, især med Hensyn til Offentlige Arbejdsskoler* (Songs for Young Girls Especially Intended for Public Work Schools, 1799) contains numerous examples of this kind of propaganda. In the preface to the collection Hjort writes that, as a "citizen of the state", he has published these songs with the aim of "spreading morality, love of work, and a more refined taste among the common people" (Hjort 1799).

One notices here an idealistically envisaged educational aim, the target group of which is not just potential recipients of poor relief but the common people as a whole. It is likewise characteristic that the goal is not only to bring about improved attitudes and characteristics, but now even more to instil aptitudes and skills.

Once again it is clear that this construction concerns bodily matters. The idea is to stimulate the readiness and willingness of the flesh. In Hjort and Bunkeflod, however, this takes place not as in Baggesen, from a sentimental standpoint but from moral aspirations. In other words, we see here a fourth variant of the view of the body. We may now try to sum up these four aspects of the new interest in the body.

The body in the searchlight

The enlightenment project of rationalism comprised not only setting up agricultural commissions, school commissions, and poverty commissions, but also gymnastics commissions, all with their attendant rules and laws in these fields. To this end there had to be a drive not just towards material reforms but also towards social reforms and changes in consciousness and attitudes. All in all, it was a matter of neither purely material nor purely idealistic motives, but of a new outlook on life and the development of a new human type, not just in the nobility and in bourgeois officialdom, but everywhere in society, although primarily among farm owners and then down to the poorest lodgers and day labourers.

The agrarian reforms were thus part of a greater disciplining and civilizing whole in the form of a restructuring not just of farm management and breeding, but also of the attitude to production. The agrarian reforms were part of a major project that comprised both external and internal nature. Not just the farm but also social life and sexual life had to be reorganized, tightened, and rationalized. Both farming operations and the management of the mind had to be brought into the sphere of culture. Or to put it another way: to make the most of the reorganization, it had to be accompanied by improvements in sex life and reforms in the sphere of social policy.

It was in this context that J.L. Reventlow included physical exercise in his enlightenment and education measures. In his *Pro Memoria* from 1794 he declares that intellect and reason are a person's primary

and most important power, and that an ability to follow the insight
of reason requires the right temperament, living emotion, and moral
mastery of "sensual drives and desire", and that diligence would here
be one of mankind's main virtues. He therefore asks rhetorically
whether both body and soul should be educated. His point is that
the soul makes "greater, more lasting, and more certain progress" if
the body is also educated and cultivated, so that school managers are
made capable of "playfully supervising, encouraging, and instructing
young people in such exercises as make the body light and supple
without depriving it of its strength".

The direct incentive to take an interest in the welfare of the body
is that hard agricultural labour makes the body heavy and stiff, which
makes the peasant's mind heavy and stiff. There are thus both general philosophical and concrete reasons underlying the suggestion to
teach physical exercise in both theory and practice. According to J.L.
Reventlow, the body should be both disciplined and stimulated:

> To educate the body, young people must be provided with physical
> work and moreover encouraged to do games and exercises. For these
> exercises one must ensure that they have the necessary room, but one
> should see to it that they are not strained beyond their strength nor
> exerted too little. (Reventlow 1794/1900: 90 f.)

We see here a distinct example of the typical rationalistic and pragmatic view that the body should be educated and refined, that the
body is the instrument of the mind, and that the education and
disciplining of the body takes place "in the service of the good
cause", in other words, that it is subordinate to things outside the
body, primarily a philosophically determined thesis: the suppleness
of the body benefits the suppleness and functioning of the mind
and of reason.

With this, modernity with its idea of progress and compensation
for the lack of civilization in former times is also expressed in the
field of bodily culture – and immediately we get the other side of
modernity: the sense of loss and the emotional-sentimental lament
of ancient innocence. This is most clearly expressed by one of the
people closest to J.L. Reventlow, namely Jens Baggesen, in his poem
Da jeg var lille (When I Was Little):

There was a time when I was very little
My body was no more than two feet long
And when I think this sweet thought, tears start flowing
And that is why I often think it now.
(Baggesen 1907: 287 f.)

What we see here is the distance of self-reflection which means that one not only *is* a body, one also *has* a body. Whether the standpoint is didactic-educational or sentimental makes no difference. In both cases there is a reflexive relation to the body, proceeding from the upright-walk attitude to the body, which now no longer exists as a *fait accompli* in raw immediacy, but on the contrary is perceived as malleable. With this distancing step, the way is open not only for the body to be reworked, it can also be reworked with style. The idea of the movement of the body and the soul, that is, the stylish plasticity and emotional diversity, makes it possible to have a conscious and reflexive attitude to having one's body available for all manner of different undertakings.

This is an enormous change of mentality taking place here in the 1790s. Pragmatism is accompanied by emotionalism, as a result of which the body is now visible as a separate entity, which can be an object for disciplining efforts and sensitiveness. The body can now be made an object of planning, design, and stylistic endeavours. The condition for this is that the body should be segregated as a special entity and that this separated body should then be disciplined in a special institutionalized framework.

The new drive to both discipline and educate differed from the pre-rationalist castigation of the flesh, by which the body was perceived as a kind of chopping block. In the old perception of the body there was no faith in, let alone knowledge of, the progress of civilization and irreversible gains in the sphere of bodily culture. Here the body was either an abode of desire or an enemy, which always deserved a beating because of its unalterable inclination to laziness, lust, and drunkenness. This perception of the permanent and static character of the body differs radically from modernity's view of the body as mobile, plastic, and mutable.

According to the pre-modern perception of the body, it could be flogged again and again: it did not help very much. This changed

with the mentality of modernity. From having been an objection-
able monster it became an occasion for intervention; despite being
placed far down on the civilization scale, raw and undeveloped, it
was seen as simultaneously equipped with rich, slumbering natural
abilities which, if one devotes sufficient attention to them, can be
made to blossom in full, and this in turn, it was held furthered the
development of the mental capacities of the individual and hence
of society as a whole.

This intervention took place, first and foremost, at schools and
in the army's military education.

The influence of Peter Villaume

Chr. Ditlev Reventlow and Johann Ludvig Reventlow who took the
initiative to the first systematic exercises for the common people
during the 1780'ies at the estates of Pederstrup in Lolland and Brahetrolleborg respectively in southern Funen were inspired by the
German philanthropic body culture (Kayser Nielsen 1993: 56 pp.).
They became acquainted with it in their early years as they were
students at Sorø Academy, where Johann Bernhard Basedow, who
fathered the German body philanthropy in Denmark, worked as a
teacher in the 1760's. When Johann Ludvig Reventlow acquired the
Brahetrolleborg estate in 1777, he began gradually to be interested
in engaging Peter Villaume from Berlin to take care of teaching
gymnastics to the brightest peasant children from the estate. However, he first succeeded in doing so in 1793.

This Villaume was not just anyone. Reventlow got hold of a
European capacity who, with a publication of a couple of hundred
pages about physical exercises, had contributed to J.H. Campe's 16-
volume education encyclopaedia *Revisionsværk*, written in 1785-91
(translated into Danish 1799-1806). This publication, which was
primarily marked by a rationalistic and distinct systematic approach,
was characteristic of Villaume's way of thinking. It described partly
the individual parts of the body, partly the individual gymnastic
exercises: Each part of the body was to be trained systematically.

Secondly, special importance was attached to moral improvements, such as "the moderation of the passions". However, it is
characteristic that the way to reach this was by going through an

"education of the body". It was thought, however, that moral improvement would not matter that much if education was not linked to the body. Only in this way would knowledge reach the "power that emphasises its learning" (Villaume 1802: 218).

The third characteristic of the theory of the early rationalistic and philanthropic body culture was the thought of cultivation. It was assumed that nature had already put up a good and strong raw material that was now to be improved. Leaving it to nature's own ability to proceed would imply surrender to a principal of chance. Instead one could meet nature and aim at an improvement of what it had made, i.e. with "the education of the body" (Villaume 1802: 193).

For that reason children should be dressed in clothes that made it possible for them to move freely, stimulating the children to play freely and not organised by adults. Another possibility was "artificial" exercises, which means constructed, systematic exercises. By this the philanthropists wished to help nature to create a "natural", supple and moderate body. The wish for improvement of the body predisposition that is given by nature partly aimed at acknowledgement, partly at superior perspectives of physical exercises in direction of civilisation and cultivation. So the conception of nature played a role directly and indirectly.

As it is said characteristically by the vicar, P.O. Boisen, who became the principal of the college of education in Lolland with C.D. Reventlow and later a bishop: "Children are not wicked by nature, but have an ability for the good" (Boisen 1800: 5).

Villaume's book, together with J.L. Reventlow's *Pro Memoria* from 1794 about the organisation of the college of education at a rationalistic and hierarchic foundation (Reventlow 1794/1900: 106), with the main emphasis laid on order, systematic and classification, are the most distinguished sources to throw light on the real philanthropically orientated body exercises in Denmark. The fundamental ideas that are repeated in these books are a rationalistic educational and informative perspective, a distinct discipline effort as well as a desire for order and classification.

This sense of "order" was for Peter Villaume and J.L. Reventlow primarily about analytic categorisation and hierarchies, while the more down-to-earth P.O. Boisen, by the word "order" understood the opposite of disorder and "simplicity". While the purpose of Villaume's and Reventlow's books was apparently to initiate gymnastics in the direction of physical activities and physical exercises, they were in fact just as much philosophical works that not only included directions of activity but also argumentation and educational reasons for these. With Boisen, however, the humanistic education thoughts went primarily in a practical direction. He was less detailed and philosophical than the others.

The sources also indicate that J.L. Reventlow had strong benefit-orientated motives with these physical exercises (if nothing else, prizes were given for diligence to those pupils who had worked particularly hard in the estate school).

From his early years in Sorø he, through Basedow, was influenced by Locke's materialistic theory of education, i.e. that the input of the senses is the basis of intellectual recognition and, consequently, in order to eliminate the factor of chance it was important to stimulate the senses and the bodily activities, when the task was to create active and diligent peasants. Such thoughts were not unfamiliar to Villaume either. He writes about the basis of the education of the soul that the soul "gets its ideas, the reason to all its operations, only by help from the body: Through the senses" (Villaume 1802: 221). The desire to create active and "vindskibelige" (industrious) peasants was an essential part of the philosophical theories.

Health and physical education in late 18th-Century Copenhagen

At that time influential circles in Copenhagen also began to be interested in systematic body movements. The leading circles here already in the 1780'ies showed interest in bodily activities in the direction of bodily civilisation. They wanted to fight the voluptuous life that was said to dominate among the Copenhagen upper class, and they also wanted to fight the common people's unruliness and coarseness. The doctor Johan Clemens Tode was the leading figure within this interest. He was the leading writer within the Danish literature on health information during this period and could swagger about having readers among the most prominent persons in Copenhagen from the royal family and the most important nobility to the most important representatives of the new trading upper class (Mellemgaard and Kayser Nielsen 1996).

Regarding the physical exercises, the important questions of the time were discussed in "educated" places as Dreyer's Club and in the literary circles of "Bakkehuset". They represented the social and intellectual places where the progressive upper class socialised with pride and joy, and where, among others, the writer Knud Lyhne Rahbek took actively part in the novel healthy outdoor movement. Altogether the desire to form and stage the body was great during this period up until about 1800. This desire was particularly stated by civil circles, dominated by landowners, theologians and philosophers who not only wished to discipline, but also to educate the body with refinement which should develop and strengthen the senses. This is, among other things, expressed in the tendency to use nature, not only as a recreation room but also as a movement room.

The longing for a more natural life was great in these educational and educated circles. Since life in the city represented the unnatural, unhealthy and disharmonious, life in the countryside or at least a periodic life in the countryside and a more natural life in the city became an ideal. The young crown prince Frederik – the later Frederik the 6th – therefore was brought up after Rousseau's principles. At the same time Frederiksberg Garden, like many other gardens of that time, changed from the stiff geometric French garden style to the sensitive, alternating, organic and romantic English Garden.

In the 1790s progressive circles of citizens started a systematic education of the body. It took place in so-called "institutes" of which Christiani's Institute in Vesterbro from 1794 is the most famous – not least because it is the background of Jens Juels' famous painting "The Running Boy" from 1799. With his portrait of a boy in the puberty running light and elegant with supple movements, this painting marks a new ideal of the body as a contrast to the stiff, almost geometric body posture of the time of courtesy. Just as the outer nature would be renewed in a more sensitive way, the human body would also be formed more supple and more sliding.

The leading figure in the breakthrough of the athletics/gymnastics in Copenhagen was V.V.F.F. Nachtegall. He started his gymnastic career in the institute that Court Chaplain Christiani had established in 1794 in the Vesterbro-district where the gymnasium, according to Nachtegall, was more often being used for informal amusement than for methodical physical exercises. We know from other sources that the "amusements" were running and swimming as well as ordinary movement pleasure, as it also appears in Jens Juels' painting of the running boy which probably was one of Christiani's pupils (Dragehjelm 1933). In 1799 Nachtegall was employed in Schouboe's Institute that had been established a year before as a competitor to Christiani's institute. However, he had more ambitious plans. In 1799 he established the Society of Gymnastics in Copenhagen where students and dealers came, and at the end of the year he took the step in full and established his own Institute of Gymnastics. Now he was ready to enter the field. The institute immediately got five pupils and before the end of the year it had 25 pupils. In a handwritten book from 1840 about the beginning of gymnastics in Copenhagen, he even claimed that "the number was more than 150 boys and juniors" (Nachtegall 1840: 3).

From the beginning Nachtegall's initiatives benefited from the fact that influential persons within politics and culture sent their children to his institute (Kayser Nielsen 1995b). He became the main character within the body culture and the history of athletics after the turn of the century, not least due to Crown Prince Frederik's keen interest in his project. It is, however, characteristic for both Nachtegall and the Prince that they were not quite as interested in the psychic-philosophical questions as the leading circles of the 1790s.

The close co-operation between Nachtegall and Crown Prince Frederik moved the body culture away from civil society into the state authority regime. In 1834 when he published his last book *Lærebog i Gymnastik til Brug for de lærde skoler i Danmark*, there is nothing about reflections of good manners, not even educational reflections. His main purpose for letting pupils in schools be trained in climbing was that it was good for preventing dizziness (!) – besides the book is mostly about swimming, drills etc.

It is striking that Nachtegall in the two works he wrote in his old age on the history of gymnastics, neglects the Reventlows and their pioneer works. He directly mentions the Vesterborg and Skaarup educational seminars and their principals' ideas that gymnastics was a subject every school teacher should know about. C.D. Reventlow was

even the "father" of the Vesterborg College of Education. He also
points out that it was to Saxtorph's merit that the Blågård College
of Education was the first school that combined methodical teaching
of physical exercises with the other teaching subjects (Nachtegall
1830: 6). He fails to mention that J.L. Reventlow had had considerable influence on the set up of Blågård College of Education in 1792.
Furthermore it is mentioned that "Count Holstein of Holsteinborg
was the first landowner in the Kingdom to introduce gymnastic
exercises in his schools" (Nachtegall 1830: 16). Not a word about
Johann Ludvig and Christian Ditlev Reventlow – even though it is
written already in the school regulations of 1791 for C.D. Reventlow's estate that physical exercises increase the strength and the
dexterity of the body and therefore should not be neglected in the
schools, and that exercises like rowing, swimming and jumping with
sticks, led by the rector P.O. Boisen, Reventlow's right hand, had
been practised at the Vesterborg College of Education (Holgaard
Rasmussen 1979: 18).

Presumably, it is not only because of tactical considerations
and the desire for making himself more important that the eldest
philanthropic demand for gymnastics was consequently neglected,
but also due to a fundamentally different conception of the "right"
physical exercises. We are dealing with a change of attitude. The
more sophisticated conception of the relation between body and soul
from the days of Lunding, J.L. Reventlow and Villaume was now
replaced by a robust devotion to the body. The interaction between
body and soul was now reduced to causality and, consequently there
was nothing to prevent the maximum development of the bodily
organs. Surely Nachtegall arranged a number of sportive swimming
contests in Copenhagen and was zealous in maximising the perform-
ances.

The Reventlow brothers had never dreamt that the physical exercises would go in that direction. The perspective of good manners
lost some of its meaning in favour of a nationalistic toned performance, and around 1810 the old "noble" philanthropic perspective was
disputed from several sides (Kayser Nielsen 1993: 63 ff.).

So eventually, the civil and locally characterised body culture
lost the battle with the military about the framework of the gymnastics. Up until 1898 the military gymnastic institute was the only

place where gymnastic teachers for public schools could be trained in Denmark. The ideas behind the introduction of the gymnastics in the Education Act stemmed from the military version of the conception of the body. The Brahetrolleborg College of Education was closed, and the Vesterborg College of Education was not able to uphold the philanthropic idea of education.

DISCIPLINE AND NATIONALISM: BODY, SPORT AND CULTURE IN 19TH CENTURY DENMARK

The lines of institutionalized Danish body culture were drawn up clearly at the turn of the 19th century: there were two different "styles" with two different ideological backgrounds and two different aims. The first one of these existed in the countryside while the other was dominant in the capital city of Copenhagen. They were in fierce competition, as the newcomer movement in Copenhagen was eager to promote its new ideas and, consequently, to oust the ideas of the older provincial movement with its roots in the Enlightenment. The purpose of this chapter, concomitantly, is to show how the militaristic body culture in the capital succeeded – thanks to unscrupulous lobbyism – in its attempts, and to show how the result of the competition between these two spheres had a considerable impact on the development of Danish body culture history, especially the influence of the Grundtvigians after 1850, who owe much to both of the aforementioned spheres.

Two body culture spheres – around 1800

In the countryside, with the educational system for the common people as forum, a humanistic education ideal with regard to the body was prevalent. It was maintained primarily by the two philanthropic noblemen and estate owners Chr. Ditlev Reventlow and Johann Ludvig Reventlow, who during the 1780s at their estates Pederstrup in Lolland and Brahetrolleborg in southern Fyn took the initiative to devise the first systematic exercises for the common people and their children (Kayser Nielsen, 1993: 37 ff.). They were inspired by the German philanthropic body culture which they became acquainted with in their early years as students at the Sorø Academy where Johann Bernhard Basedow, who fathered the German body philanthropy in Denmark, worked in the 1760s. The sources tell us that already in 1782 Chr. Ditlev Reventlow arranged "amusing games" for the peasants around Pederstrup (Reventlow 1902: 70) and that one Sunday, shortly after midsummer 1787, Johann Ludvig Reventlow arranged dances and games for the peasants and their children in the gardens of his castle (Peitersen 1973: 11).

The leading figure in the breakthrough of gymnastics in Copenhagen was V.V.F.F. Nachtegall. Whilst the Reventlows tried to promote physical exercise through teachers' colleges and village schools, i.e. through channels created by civil society, Nachtegall used the more military and national channels. An unscrupulous opportunist with an elaborated sense of lobbyism, he felt that his methods opened more doors to success than merely promoting PE in the teachers' colleges. His first book, an instruction for teachers in the army, was published in 1805. Its contents were directed towards the education of "warriors". The book was not exactly typical for the reflections of Enlightenment in that the didactic purposes of the Age of Enlightenment were completely neglected.

Admittedly, Nachtegall was not the only one in the capital who wrote educational books about gymnastics and physical exercise. His colleague P.H. Mønster, the principal of the School of Posterity, also did that kind of work. But his great work from 1804 about the use of gymnastics in the education of youth differed very much from the intentions of Nachtegall. This work was totally in the spirit of Villaume-Reventlow and was definitely marked by philanthropic and philosophical ideals of education. However the book dealt only slightly with practical things in connection with the education and was more about upbringing than technique. The same goes for his book from 1803 about swimming. In this book he did not mention the military as a background for the sport but claimed instead that physical power would be encouraged if one followed "the doctor's and the philosopher's advice, as well as the teacher's complete advice" (Mønster 1803: 4). The same Mønster resigned in 1805 from the progressive *Efterslægtens School* in order to be a rector in the village of Gyrstinge in Sjælland and saw to it that gymnastics was taught in the schools of the parish. – This "escape" to the countryside is symbolic: Copenhagen was "a lost case" for militaristic educational purposes. And when in 1814 the new Education Act for compulsory school attendance was issued, it was evident that the martial and nationalistic "tone" was prevalent.

At the Blågård College of Education, Nachtegall started in 1805 to give lectures on the theory and the methodology of gymnastics.

According to him, the students here distinguished themselves particularly in "swimming and military exercises" (Nachtegall 1831: 9).
Here we can see a clear difference between the state military initiatives and the conception based on the civil society schools of the
countryside. Without doubt, Nachtegall himself had nothing against
teachers being educated to teach gymnastics in the village schools,
but he favoured their being educated in the military regimes – on
which he could keep a firm hand. As King Frederik VI felt the same
about the matter, it was made possible for civilians to have access to
free education at the military Institute of Gymnastics (Nachtegall
1831: 12). Although educated in a Rousseauian spirit, the King was
deeply interested in the new militaristic body activities. His enthusiasm was reciprocated by Nachtegall who, in 1831, dedicated his
book *Gymnastikkens fremgang i Danmark* (The progress of gymnastics
in Denmark) to the King, but it was not only the royal court that
found Nachtegall's message appealing, but also other prominent
people in the highest cultural circles in Copenhagen (Nachtegall
1820). To give the impression that he was a nodal point in the
capital's Establishment, it was extremely important for Nachtegall
to mention in a letter to the philosopher and novelist F.C. Sibbern
that the King would be present when his pupils performed their
skills (Nachtegall 1832).

The consequences of Nachtegall's victory

The introduction from above of a military form of gymnastics in
the Danish peasant schools from 1814 probably contributed considerably to the establishment of a Danish 'dual public' – consisting
on the one hand of a state-oriented sphere, and on the other of a
civil sphere – with its political and cultural conflicts that became
so characteristic for Danish society during the second half of the
19th century. The dual public feature was a distinctive aspect of
Danish society until the between-war-years and was not finally
defeated until the great compromise between city and country in
political, social, and cultural areas took place in Denmark as well as
in Finland and all the Nordic countries in the 1930s, and which was
finally codified by virtue of the municipal reform in 1970 (Kayser
Nielsen 1997d).

However, it must be pointed out that this hegemonic fight
was never a serious threat to the coherence of the Danish society
throughout the period. As we shall see below the common nationalistic intentions of both the two public spheres rendered a fundamental disruption impossible, while at the same time the state never
intended to annihilate the civil sphere. This sphere on the other hand
could never have dreamt of establishing a disloyal counterweight to
the state.

That said, it is also clear that from around the middle of the 19th
century and onwards, a certain tension between the ambitions of
the two public spheres was prevalent, not least on the local level. As
Erik Nørr has shown, the conflict between the local administration
and the state administration manifested itself primarily in the area
of school matters. This conflict in particular became worse after the
introduction of parish councils from 1842, where it did not suit the
mean farmers in the parish councils to become reconciled with the
central institutions of education (Nørr 1994: 31 ff.).

However, there is no doubt that the seeds to this conflict were
sown earlier, partly in the events that preceded the Education Act
of 1814 – especially the forced body-culture initiatives, and partly in
the actual legal administration of the 1814 Education Act with regard
to the area of gymnastics. Here we have a rare and clear example of
the fact that the history of sport can actually contribute to history
at large.

If Nachtegall had not succeeded in ousting the philanthropic
idea of the proper body culture for farmers' children and substitut-
ing it with his militaristic gymnastics – resembling the much-hated
monthly drill of the farmer-soldier behind the church on Sunday
afternoons (Holmgaard 1986: 44 ff.) – farmers would probably
not have felt the same reluctance towards the martial gymnastics
of the state schools, for which there is some evidence (Korsgaard
1986: 34 ff.). In continuation of this, had this antagonism not been
common, it would have been much more difficult for the Grundtvigians to maintain their new civil and voluntary body culture after
1850. This holds true especially after 1870 when the political disagreement between the aristocratic government and the king, on
the one side, and the farmers on the other, escalated.

A contra-factual question

The peasant schools' teaching of gymnastics was – thanks to the energetic efforts of Nachtegall and King Frederik 6th in particular – shaped by military lines of direction, while the supervision was put into the hands of the clergy: the bishop at the top and, under him, a school commission with a vicar as the central point. They had only a sparse understanding of athletics, if any, and therefore they were not capable of defying the military idea of gymnastics. In time with the fact that the thoughts of the philanthropic humanistic education from the turn of the 19th century had faded out of sight, more and more was put into the hands of the individual teacher. Therefore, as a safety precaution the Ministry of Cultural Affairs introduced a special professional inspection of the gymnastics. The gymnastics inspector should, among other things, make some comments on the reports that were sent from the deaneries every year (Nørr 1994: 363 ff.).

Unfortunately we know hardly anything about what gymnastics was really like in the municipal schools before 1848, when the inspections began. Statements concerning the number of capable teachers are insufficient. Maybe the teachers' lack of gymnastic experience resulted in more easygoing and amusing sessions than we can imagine. Or, on the other hand, perhaps this same lack of experience meant that the teachers stuck to the most simple method: to drill and command. And if the latter was the case it is possible to refer to Nachtegall's recipe where there is a host of instructions. If we are to judge the teaching form in the so-called "mutual teaching" that both Nachtegall and Frederik 6th were particularly fond of (Nachtegall 1828), there was no lack of marching in the schools where this teaching form was practised (Høybye-Nielsen 1969: 42 ff.). It is reasonable to see a correspondence between the general form of this model of teaching and gymnastic teaching in particular, especially considering the fact that Nachtegall in his 1828 book on gymnastics recommended the mutual teaching model.

Conversely, one could ask what might have happened to the farmers' aversion to these physical exercises if an education of philanthropic conviction had marked gymnastics in the Danish peasant schools from 1814? Unfortunately it is not possible to answer this question, but there is reason to believe that it must have been rather difficult for the strong Danish Grundvigian movement, with its lighter view of the body, to gain a breakthrough when later in the 19th century they introduced the Swedish Ling system of gymnastics with its philanthropic, educational ideals.

As has been pointed out, Grundtvig himself was always reluctant to pay homage to those people and ideas that had influenced him most (Vind 1999: 59). Grundtvig himself visited the University of Copenhagen from 1800-1803, i.e. in those formative years where the new ideas of the body were influential and were later taught at the very same Schoubo Institute where Nachtegall had tried his first ideas, but had left in order to substitute rationalism with militarism. Per Henrik Ling, the founder of the Swedish gymnastic system, also stayed in Copenhagen (together with his son) during the years 1801-1804 (Werlauf 1873/74: 272). Later in the 19th century the Swedish gymnastic system was to be the Grundtvigians' icon in sport and body culture.

So, there is some reason to agree with the statement that the characteristic dual-organized education initiatives and information initiatives "do not come from the Grundtvigian philosophy" (Stenius 1993: 193). They go back much further, to the conflict between the Danish rationalistic information initiatives, and the militaristic initiatives where Nachtegall and Frederik 6th played an important role. The Grundtvigian tradition of good and evil owes a great deal to these two men. Primarily it was due to them that Danish peasants – through gymnastic classes in the state schools – came to learn the military drill for themselves – thereby acquiring a tacit knowledge of the State's view of the human body.

The Grundtvigian intention

The rifle movement in Denmark began in 1861, but the foundation was laid earlier. While the inspiration came from England at first, the idea appeared already just after the Three-Year-War (1848-50) against Slesvig-Holstein, but the idea of a volunteering "people's army" was already introduced in 1848. Not least Grundtvig was a passionate opponent of the standing army and wanted to replace it with a voluntary army of the "people". He declared that subscription was tantamount to slavery, whereas volunteering was an act of freedom (Korsgaard 1982: 49). Accordingly, he strived to combine the national and the democratic aspects in order to politicize the question, whereas the right-wing wanted the army to remain above political issues.

Grundtvig, however, also related these national-democratic ideas to education. His idea was that if the school, as an educational institution, was to be of benefit to the common people, it must not only give priority to intellectual activity but also deal with real life, first and foremost by way of experience. This raised the possibility of a body culture in schools that attached more importance to play and games than drill and goose step. These ideas were all combined in the wish to create a sound national soul in a sound national body, as proclaimed by Professor Sommer in 1846 (Korsgaard 1986: 36). Grundtvig's ideal, which was seen full-fledged in his famous *Prologue to the Mythology of Norden* (1832) was to raise the common people's culture and self-awareness – it is tempting to use the word reflexivity – above the level of, in his words, "animals". This civilizatoric wish to eradicate the "animalistic" mark on peasants and common people was intended to be fulfilled through the medium of education by teachers who were more inclined to *convince* than *thrash* their pupils.

Included in this was, not least, the aim of self-discipline in order to learn to put one's mind and body at the service of one's country; i. e. an intention that stemmed from a strategy of acculturation in line with the learning of language and national culture (Riordan and Krüger 1999: ix). The Grundtvigian project eventually took into consideration not only nationalism, democracy and education, but also acculturation and civilization – all in the spirit of the philanthropic Enlightenment with its emphasis on education and pedagogical means.

The rifle movement

Inspired by the national revival caused by the victory in the above mentioned war, as well as by the introduction of the June constitution in 1849 and by the National-liberal Party's politics during these years – and Grundtvig's ideas – an increased will to defend the nation arose in the upper classes. It seemed that Denmark was populated by a "people" and not just the King's patriotic subjects. H.V. Bissen's monument of "The country soldier" in the town of Fredericia is the visible symbol of this national turning-point.

During the Three Year War (1848-50) ordinary and equal compulsory military service was introduced. From this point the idea of the introduction of a voluntary corps that could support the army was not far away. But what was meant by army? Was it a standing army of the state, or an army of the people? And which role should be given to the voluntary corps? A certain dislike is noticed in the parliamentary debates of the 1850s against such corps, especially among the peasants' representatives. However, the National-liberal upper class organization still had power to maintain a generally positive attitude in the leading circles towards such a corps, provided it did not imply a role in the arming of the people.

The releasing factor was an article in Carl Ploug's national liberal daily *Fædrelandet* ("The homeland") on January 19th, 1861 by Artillery Captain, Hans Peter Valdemar Mønster about the English voluntary rifle clubs whose purpose was to disseminate knowledge about shooting and the use of arms through active exercises. In Mønster's opinion they were examples for Denmark to follow. But he did not approve of the Grundtvigian idea of a voluntary military corps, erected in the name of the people. His idea, rather, was a voluntary corps meant to provide preparatory training for the standing army. A number of well-known persons from the military, university, industry, newspaper world and literature were co-writers, including Carl Ploug himself. Therefore it was obvious that Mønster appealed to the public for support for the idea. There appeared to be great interest, and during 1861 it became so popular that the first rifle clubs started up already at the beginning of that year.

Especially decisive was the fact that already from February 1861 the project was put in a firm organization al frame through a Central Committee for the establishment of rifle clubs. But of no less importance was the fact that the case from the very beginning benefited economically from the great public interest (Kayser Nielsen 1989a). The person who seriously took up the case was the leading National-liberal politician, Orla Lehmann, who felt that rifle clubs as such belonged in the state budget. Support did not become less when Lehmann was appointed Home Secretary in September 1861.

Specifically, the rifle clubs had three problems to solve. First, the question of where shooting could take place: In Copenhagen the problem was solved by the War Minister who permitted the rifle club people the use of the Army's shooting ranges at *Englandsværn* in *Vesterbro*. The rifle clubs and the military were to share the expenses. In the countryside the farmers allowed the rifle club people to use their fields as shooting ranges.

Another problem was that of instruction. This problem was rectified surprisingly fast by the publication of a handbook on *Instructions for the Use of Weapons*, and by the summer of 1861 shooting exercises had also been organized. This handbook was supported economically from above, as the War Ministry – by request of the rifle movement's central committee – paid 100 *rigsdaler* so that it could be published all over the country.

Finally there was the question of guns and ammunition. Since Mønster did not expect any support from the state, he applied to the local authorities, the local rifle clubs and the richest landowners. However it never became a great success as there were only positive reactions in Vejle, Silkeborg and Middelfart (Krogh 1911: 57). In the town of Vejle three gentlemen from the local rifle club donated a sum of money to buy 8-10 rifles (Jensen 1968: 7). As it happened, the state supported the case actively. The Central Committee applied to the Home Secretary for the sum of 2000 *rigsdaler*. This was granted already in January 1862 with the proviso that the rifle movement also contributed with the same amount of money and that the Home Secretary was informed about which rifles they intended to buy. Furthermore, Home Secretary Lehmann sent out a circular to the county prefects in which he asked them to encourage the local rifle cause, but it was only after a reminder had been sent out in 1863 that something happened. During that year rifle clubs were established in about 100 parishes all over the country. Finally the active policy of the government gave results, as the state showed itself to be the motivating power behind the spreading of the rifle cause.

Otherwise, 1869 was the breakthrough year with regard to the establishment of rifle clubs all over the country. Here we should keep in mind that Denmark's defeat by the Germans in 1864 had been very expensive. Economically the war had cost Denmark 60 million *rigsdaler*. More than 3000 men had been killed in the war; the three duchies had been surrendered, and more than 200,000 Danes were left south of the border at "Kongeåen". Consequently thoughts of revenge were ubiquitous and a lot of banners from that time carried the lines *Northern Sleswig won back; that is the aim of the fight* ("Sønderjylland vundet, det er Kampens Maal"). This thought was kept alive especially because of the disagreement between the two states Germany and Austria, who had defeated Denmark in 1864, and the tense situation between Germany and France. The Army Law of 1867 was visible proof of these hopes. It was supposed to secure strong field-forces that could help a "Great Power" that was the enemy of Germany in the event of war. As several politicians as well as personalities within the world of culture – among others N.F.S. Grundtvig – did not like the idea of compulsory military service, but favoured the idea of a strong defence, the voluntary rifle movement became an alternative.

This rearmament, including the dreams of revenge, made the rifle movement very successful. Possibly it was also a contributing factor to the repertoire being enlarged, as during the first years – besides shooting – there were also drills and marching exercises in the schedule. The thought was that those who visited the shooting range could just as well spend their time rationally. However these exercises were not popular with the peasants as they were reminded of the drills, referred to earlier, which they hated so much.

It was hardly surprising, therefore, that the drills were soon supplemented with less martial gymnastic exercises and other forms of physical exercises. In 1868 the rifle movement's committee of Vejle Amt (county) sent out a note to the local rifle clubs ordering them to exercise shooting, gymnastic and drills. Concerning gymnastics, they recommended exercises in walking and running as well as high jump and long jump, buck jump and skipping, i.e. a combination of athletics and gymnastics.

With the handbook *Haandbog i Gymnastik for Delingsformænd ved Amts-Skytteforeningerne*, which First Lieutenant V. La Cour had compiled, there was a good basis for the exercises. In 1869 the War Ministry granted 200 *rigsdaler* to this book. The state subsidy for the athletic movement entered a new phase. Not only was shooting subsidized, but also gymnastics and instructor activities. In Fredericia, at the end of 1870s, a school of gymnastics was established for young people from 10-15 years old, who practised for two hours, twice a week. Very quickly there were more than 100 pupils who were trained by two first lieutenants from the local garrison (Jensen 1968: 14). This development was not unique. Gymnastics became more and more popular and from around 1880 many sport associations only practised gymnastics (Gjøde Nielsen 1994: 34).

So, eventually the Grundtvigian idea of a voluntary, non-military people's movement had its victory, but it is evident that this could not have happened without the strong support of the state and government. The dual public sphere of folk high schools for the farmers, and voluntary clubs – which after 1870 became even more Grundtvigian – on the one hand, and the aristocracy, civil servants and the capital's high-brow culture on the other, were to become a typical characteristicon for Denmark from around 1870, but still under the supremacy of the state's financial support.

The rifle movement between left and right in the 1880s

For the remainder of the 19th century, subsidies to the rifle movement and gymnastic movement continued, also in the turbulent "Provisional years" during the 1880s when Denmark was governed by provisional laws issued by the right-wing Prime Minister Estrup. At the beginning of the 1880s the state subsidy to the rifle movement was 20,000 Danish crowns (DKK) per year and this amount was increased hereafter, so that in 1885 it became 35,000 DKK (Kayser Nielsen 1989b: 29). This amount is remarkable, as it was given in the same year as the left wing took over power in the rifle movement. It was now led by a new Grundtvigian board, where some right wing officers sat "hostage". Nevertheless, the right wing government did not change the subsidies. Therefore, the "myth" about the "evil estate-owner" Estrup and his government's rabid persecution of the left wing does not hold true in this area.

One year later in 1886 the situation escalated: The reason was the politicization stemming from the "rifle provision" and the so-called "muzzle circular" against teachers criticizing the government. The "rifle provision" banned imports, purchase, distribution and practise in the operation of the rifles, while the muzzle circular gave title to discharge school teachers who were active in the rifle clubs. The "rifle provision" also implied that rifle clubs should have the permission of the prefect of the "amt" (county) to practise shooting. All these initiatives were met with resentment and bitterness, and in the middle of the 1880s the political situation was rather tense. On 6th September 1886, the situation culminated with the renowned encounter at Brønderslev Market between a crowd of people and the Estrup gendarmes. This disturbance was more the result of a common scuffle, however, than that of political manifestation (Pedersen and Kjeldsen 1993).

In Vejle Amt the case gained momentum, resulting in consequences on a national level. A number of rifle clubs in Vejle Amt had taken part in a celebration in Kolding for the left- wing leader Christen Berg, who had just finished a prison term he had been serving as a consequence of the rifle troubles. The right-wing people of the Central Committee wanted to give these rifle men a reprimand, but they never got the chance to do so, as the majority of the liberals, and hereafter the Right resigned. A number of rifle clubs in Vejle Amt followed their example and started a "new" rifle movement, resulting in two rifle movements from 1886.

Subsidies from the state still did not change. Both the "old" movement that was led by the Left and the Grundtvigian "Folk High School Movement", as well as the "new" right-wing movement, had a part in the subsidies. The amount of 34,000 DKK was shared with two-thirds to the Liberals and one-third to the right wing. The rifle movement and organized athletics in the form of gymnastics were regarded as "a national affair" and thus concern for them was more important than political conflicts. In 1893 the conflict between the Liberals and right wing calmed down, partly due to the Grundtvigian lobbyists whose cause it was to have state subsidies increased to 40,000 DKK per year (Kayser Nielsen 1989b: 31).

Although there were two public spheres: cultural and political, both of these were ultimately dependent on the mercy of the state. As the Norwegian sociologist Dag Østerberg pointed out, it is difficult to write the political and cultural history of the Nordic countries without taking Hegel into consideration (Østerberg 1997). But, hopefully, it is also evident that if Nachtegall and Frederik 6th had not ousted the philanthropic body culture, there would not have been more than one sphere. In the Grundtvigian non-militaristic movement, the human and rationalistic ideas of Villaume and the Reventlow brothers about how the institutionalized body culture should be performed did actually survive – with state support.

The "poor" sport

It is tempting here to make comparisons with other types of physical exercises at that time: competition sport – including cricket, football, track and field, boxing, sailing, rowing, etc. did not get proportional support from the state during the 1880s and 1890s. Certainly the First International Gymnastics and Athletics gathering in Copenhagen in 1898, in which wrestlers and boxers, as well as cricketers and football players participated, was given 10,000 DKK from the state budget of 1898/99, and likewise the Municipality of Copenhagen gave 4,000 DKK (Hansen 1995: 61). It was the first time that another kind of sport, other than rifle shooting or gymnastics, was given a subsidy. Hereafter nothing happened until 1903 when the "Dansk Idræts Forbund" – DIF (Danish Sports Federation), which was founded in 1896 was given 3,000 DKK by the state, in spite of the fact that there were an estimated 250 sports clubs in the country at that time (Jørgensen 1995a: 83). The subsidies given to the other forms of sport never reached the level of those allotted to shooting and gymnastics. Likewise, the subsidies to DIF were only about 35,000 DKK in 1938 (Jørgensen 1995b: 117, which were less than the amount allotted the rifle movement and gymnastics movement in 1893! Fortunately, subsidies increased a great deal later on, and in 1945 DIF obtained three times the amount received in 1938.

Altogether it appears that up until World War II, the state took greatest interest in the rifle and gymnastic movements, while the other sport activities had to fend for themselves. The many ball clubs established around 1900 were forced to be self-sufficient as they were not regarded as national educational organizations. On the whole it was uncertain what these modern sports represented. Many people considered them to be a passing whim that was being realized by immature louts, while the rifle and gymnastic movements were regarded as serious activities as they were both pro-national

and character-forming. Also these other forms of sport had the dis-
advantage of lacking party-political support, something which rifle
shooting and gymnastics did not. The right looked very kindly upon
shooting in particular, while the Liberals had primarily a positive
view of gymnastics, which in the form of the so-called "Swedish"
gymnastics was a political-symbolic representation for the Grundtvigian peasantry. Juxtaposed a body culture with this kind of striking
political-cultural power, other branches of sport appeared partly to
be phenomena of the city, and partly the monkey tricks of misled
young people.

The state's neglect of modern sport was not a special Danish
phenomenon. In all the European countries, the state displayed
a lack of interest in modern sports, whereas gymnastics, physical
and military training was favoured. In Denmark, however, this was
exacerbated by the special Danish history of body culture with two
national body movements, each of which served the interests of the
state.

Conclusion

Physical education as an organized body-leisure culture emerged
in Denmark at the end of the 18th century, inspired by the philanthropic movement in Europe. During the early 19th century a
nationalistic trend was annexed to it, promoted not least by the
King. Later in the century it was organized as a civil movement that,
nevertheless, was strongly subsidized by the government and parliament. On the one hand it functioned as a combination of discipline,
acculturation and education, and on the other, the liberation of the
body that began at the end of the 18th century. The Danish national
state took an interest in bodily activities in order to discipline and
control peoples' leisure time, but also to promote a devoted and
happy population. Farsighted politicians and leaders understood that
body culture was a short cut to creating both diligent and nation-
committed citizens. So, the state had a keen interest in constructing
national(istic) leisure by means of body culture.

Consequently, a great deal of the development of Danish 19th-
century society was made up of this combination of discipline and
education and the liberation of the body, which were part of the

construction of a national(istic) society and the process of individualization. Both had bodily experiences of compulsion and controlled desire as a crucial point. While this also held true on a general
European level, there were differences from country to country. In
Denmark, as in the other Nordic countries, it is evident that the
national state used and actively subsidized these activities. For these
reasons, research into the history of the civilization of the body is
a relevant field – but also a neglected field. This research into body
history and its impact on political and cultural history – including
leisure – is now underway.

DECADENCE AND VITALITY: SPORT AND THE COLLECTIVE MENTALITY AROUND 1900

The time around 1900 in Denmark, as elsewhere in Europe, was characterized by paradoxes and conflicting tendencies. This was the period in history when people spoke of *fin de siècle* and of *Jugendstil* or *art nouveau*.

On the one hand they believed that the world was heading for destruction, that they were living in the final days, that the European countries were becoming decadent and degenerate (Kayser Nielsen 1994b), and that the pillars of the nineteenth century – the nation, the family, and the cultured individual – were collapsing. It is symptomatic that the Danish health journal *Dansk Sundhedstidende* in 1896 published an article with the heading "Are we weaker than our ancestors?", in which a doctor, using the evidence of modern science, felt obliged to challenge all those pessimists who believed that mankind was on the path to ruin. He reassured readers that the average height of conscripts was now at least half an inch more than it had been a generation before (J.C. 1896a). In the same journal in the same year, however, the same doctor wrote about the risk of infection on trams, urging scrupulous hygiene: one must wash one's hands before every meal, and one must never put one's fingers in one's mouth (J.C. 1896b). In short, the time around 1900 was a time of worry. People felt that they were more or less in danger wherever they went. Mankind was in a vulnerable position in which it was necessary to protect oneself.

On the other hand, it was also the time when the "new men" (and women) sensed the dawn of better things. The world seemed to be opening up, social and political opportunities were growing, and vigorous new social classes appeared to be on the advance. Despite their rough exterior they were healthy and full of go; all they needed was to be "cultivated". The nineteenth century thus seemed to be heading for destruction, but there were also signs in the stars that a strong, vigorous, and above all young generation was ready to breathe new life in the degeneration.

We have now singled out one of the three crucial concepts that were to point the way out of the bleakness and the gloomy sense of decline and decadence – namely, the concept of youth. In the 1890s the young were appointed to solve the problem of entering the twentieth century with a new strength. People put their faith in youth. Youth – both as the abstract concept of youthfulness and in the sense of young people – was perceived as the standard-bearer of the future. Youth was believed to contain the energy that was lacking in the times. Let us look more closely at this.

The cult of youth

We are indebted to the Swedish historian Henrik Berggren for pointing out the enormous significance of the concept of youth in the years around 1900 (Berggren 1995). This applied all over Europe, and Scandinavia did not lag behind by any means. Youth became a vogue word in the public debate, in which educationalists and philosophers such as G. Stanley Hall, Ellen Key, and Nietzsche were leading lights in the dissemination of the youth gospel.

At the same time, youth became an object for public planning and care. Changes in franchise, the introduction of compulsory military service, and the reorganization of grammar-school education (in Denmark in 1903, in Norway in 1896, in Sweden in 1905) with a growing, Spencer-inspired emphasis on practical and nationally oriented subjects instead of a dusty classical education – all pointed in the direction of a concern for the societal significance of youth (Meinander 1994: 48 ff.). The existing political and religious movements acquired youth sections, and completely new and independent youth organizations arose, based on the English scouts and the German *Wandervögel*. Visible proof of this organization of young people was, among others, the YMCA, which had come to Denmark back in 1878 as a way to modernize traditional Christian youth work. Another was the Danish Youth Clubs. The origin of this part of the "popular" Danish tradition of enlightenment dates back to 1887, to Nørre Åby in western Fyn, where the Grundtvigian Free School teacher Olaf Nielsen founded a youth club. This quickly met a response in the surrounding parishes. In the Kolding district, too, a similar movement began, likewise with Grundtvigian inspiration, but not until around 1896. Seven years later, the association of Danish Youth Clubs (De danske Ungdomsforeninger, DdU) was founded in 1903 at a meeting in Fredericia. Fourty clubs joined together and thereby comprised some 3,000 members, based especially in Fyn and eastern Jutland (Bruhn 1979: 42 ff.).

In this connection, however, a dilemma was encountered. While adults appreciated the vitality and freshness of youth, they also feared its unruly nature. On the one hand, they wished to let youthful energy take the place of weakness and laxity, but on the other hand they wanted to keep a tight rein on matters so that they did not get out of hand. Here, however, a new problem arose: could young people's vitality be expressed if there was too much control from the top? Many people involved in popular enlightenment and child-rearing doubted this. They wanted to do no more than "arrange things" for the young people and then let them act as independently as possible (Kayser Nielsen 1993: 129 ff.). Olaf Nielsen from Nørre Åby summed up this liberal attitude as follows:

> Let us for the sake of the young people not be too hard about danc-ing any more than about a game of cards, which after all does not hurt anyone, for dancing is a part of youth… We do not wish to see young people with old people's habits, which is the most dismal sight imaginable. (Højskolebladet 1894/48: 1449)

The great task was therefore to create forms that could satisfy both the needs of youth as young people and society's need to impose a certain degree of regulation and to ensure that this regulation was not so strict as to confine the self-expression of youth. Otherwise, instead of having young people as the salvation of the human race, one would be back where one started. The age required conventions and organizations that could satisfy both individual and communal needs. Yet there was another factor in the picture: movement.

The cult of movement

The other crucial concept in the faith in youth as a way out of the morass of decadence and degeneration was movement. It too summed up several different aspects and phenomena characteristic of the time around 1900, in that it was used in a wide range of dif-ferent areas as an interpretative matrix. This concept intertwined a large number of threads. Let us take a look at a few of them.

One of the books that had a massive impact on turn-of-the-century Denmark was Claus Lambek's *Verdsligt Aandsliv hos Folket* ("Secular mentality of the People"). With his attempt to take the temperature of the social climate and the mentality of the times, he gives us insight into the way people thought then. It is symptomatic that Lambek advocates the view that stillness, rest, and indolence are evil, while physical and mental movement was the goal to aim for: "Stagnation is lifeless, while everything of value for the mind comes from movement" (Lambek 1906: 13). In other words, movement is life and life is movement.

A view like this was able to gain a hearing in a phase of social history characterized by a breach with accustomed traditions and a huge migration from the countryside to the expanding towns and cities. Many people had the challenge of adjusting to the speed of urban life with its many changing sensory impressions, many gazes, and many bodily encounters with people in the streets. Movement – with body and soul.

In other contexts too, movement was seen as the great solution. In late nineteenth-century France there was active research into the phenomenon of memory. The gradually prevailing view was that memory was not stored data but the ability to arrange, structure, organize, cite, and recite impressions from the past. In other words, the crucial thing was said to be the ability of the brain to make movements between these impressions and combine them into new wholes. In the same way, the ability to write was perceived as the ability of the brain to get the fingers in motion, so that the arm, the hand, and the fingers were felt to be as important as the brain for remembering how to write (Matsuda 1996: 79 ff.). The truth about these matters is not relevant here. The point – characteristic of the times – is that these phenomena were conceived in a universe of motion, and the category of movement became the matrix for understanding them.

In nutritional science too, movement was a crucial concept. One of the main problems for people who did not have to struggle to obtain their food was constipation. The cure for this, it was believed, was to activate the digestion. Proper food alone was not enough; the decisive factor was how food affected the metabolism. The metabolic rate, and hence the movement and exchange between the food, the intestines, and the combustion process, was all-important (Schmidt and Kristensen 1986: 170 ff.). This aspect of life was thus also interpreted through categories of movement.

The desire for hardening – in moderation

We saw above that the time around 1900 was perceived as a time of danger when one had to protect oneself. This view has its impact on the body, leading to a desire to harden oneself, to acquire a coat of armour with which to resist both one's own physical weakness and the surrounding world. In the dynamic youthful society, in which every opportunity seemed to be open, it was evidently necessary to enclose oneself in a tough body. This was the opposite of traditional agrarian society with its small closed enclaves, where the body was an open body: here people all ate gladly from the same dish and did not care what came out of the other end of the body. Peasant society knew nothing of self-discipline when it came to breaking wind.

Now things changed. The more open society became, the greater was the need to keep the body in check. It was a question of not being overrun (Vidler 1994). The crucial problem was the relation between the individual and the collective, with the individual's bodily limits being one of the central questions. How could one ensure that the individual maintained his boundaries – his "armour" – without the skull becoming so hard that the world cannot penetrate it? Where was the boundary between inner strength and being closed to the world? And where could one find spheres in society where one could have training in the creation of such a harmonious balance between the individual and the collective – and also training in physical sense, so that the balance between individual self-fulfilment and subordination to the community would become a physical experience, a kind of tacit knowledge that would leave its mark as physical paths in the mind? These were some of the questions highlighted around 1900, on the boundary between the old century with its worship of authority, "law", and control, and the new century which saw an onrushing and self-assured individualism demanding the right of free expression.

Johannes V. Jensen and the new formal vitalism

If one had to point to a Dane who, more than anyone else, represents the transition between the nineteenth and the twentieth centuries, it must be the author Johannes V. Jensen, who was awarded the Nobel Prize for literature in 1944. He sums up the familiarity with the spleen and decay of the 1890s and the vitalistic hero-worship in the first optimistic decade and a half of the twentieth century, the time up to 1914 and the shocking realization that progress does not last. At the same time, Jensen reflects the fundamental faith in both youth and motion, just as he was obsessed by the youth sports movement. There is therefore good reason for choosing him as the figure that illuminates the collective mentality and the social climate around 1900.

Johannes V. Jensen made his debut as a writer in the 1890s, and as a student in Copenhagen in the middle of the *fin de siècle* decade this veterinary surgeon's son suffered every imaginable torment and trouble. His first novels, which he later repudiated, are deeply marked by the spectre of degeneration, dominated as they are by compulsive pondering, dreaminess, and powerless youths.

During the first decades of the twentieth century he overcame this trauma. Yet his earlier experiences are perhaps the real reason why he so dramatically turned in the direction of the new gospel of movement. Yet even in this most vitalistic of all Danish authors of the time, we can see an emphasis on the form in the midst of all the fascination with movement and its significance for the construction of a mental personal untouchability – a *noli me tangere* stance. Some quotations from his work may serve as illustration. In *Mit Forår* ("My Spring") from 1901 we read:

> *A wind blew over me in my young years, I became restless, it was my destiny. I fled to outdistance time, but time beat me on the finishing straight. ... Whistles storm above my head, I raise the glass in my hand and establish a private well-being... A toast to the unquench-able appetite.*

This thematizes how he came to terms with the bewilderment that threatens to isolate the individual who is unable to come into harmony with his times, and this harmony succeeds best if one is vital, if one has an appetite for life. If one has this one can certainly manage as a loner. As a part of a movement that is greater than himself he becomes strong and has an opportunity to develop his innermost strength: the thirst for life that can never be quenched. This is even clearer in his little book about Kipling from 1912, where he writes that "the mobile and the distant attract me more than the introverted and fermenting".

Yet what is mobile requires form or else the result will be chaotic and diffuse. In the poem *Afsked* ("Departure", 1902) the narrator invokes the steady, time-keeping beat of a heart as a means to regulate an otherwise oceanic overflowing energy which can appear uncontrollable and even dangerous to health (Jensen 1954: 37):

> *I have longed for the beat, the beat*
> *of an unassailably pumping heart.*
> *Yet how I have striven to be stripped bare*
> *of the strength that feeds my sensitivity,*
> *– Oh I have a little of my health! –*
> *and of the gigantic energy*
> *with which deep down I am bored to death.*

In the myth *Haabets første Dag* ("The First Day of Hope", 1901) he is less explicit, but the basic idea cannot be mistaken. He is in Oslo when the thaw is just coming. There is snow and ice on the streets, while people are screwing up their eyes at the sun. The streets feel closed in, but at the same time pigeons fly over the roofs like the swallows in Cadiz. There are workmen hacking at ice, and a young Jewess passes by. In short, things seem incoherent. But a locomotive is standing in the station. It provides the outward force while simultaneously – restrained by form – it is in control of its energy. Jensen is on the way to becoming a machine-man, but he still does not forget the corporeal and unpredictable dimension of life. The coordination of form and force is the great task here, around 1900, for him, as for so many others. He gives words to the *Zeitgeist*, the spirit of the time; better than most people, he has an eye for paradoxes and contrasts, as when he once wrote about the people of Salling that they "sang strivingly when they spoke" (Jensen 1962: 101). In *Den ny Verden* ("The New World", 1907) he wrote that it is not enough to be born with strength: "More is needed for the development of what is in the body". One must "make a system" (Jensen 1907: 244): So, the third crucial concept is form.

More clearly than anywhere else, this is seen in the death-portrait of his hero or anti-hero (who knows?) Mikkel Thøgersen in the novel *Kongens Fald* (The Fall of the King), 1900-1:

Mikkel's poor head was like a cast object which had spent seventy years in the mould before it could be cooled and finished. For seventy years his face was liquid, reflecting the thousand expressions of life, his eyes were like living metal catching the light. (Jensen 1963: 199).

The sense of motion (in the nerves) is the true feeling of life in him. Above all, Mikkel senses movement and connected movements: speed, confrontation, flows of people, and so on. Yet all in a form or mould, so that energy and form can influence each other in a life-giving tension. His death, as is clear from the quotation, is synonymous with the form gaining the upper hand. Death is pure form and petrified movement.

Johannes V. Jensen finds a life like this, with its combination of form and energy, in modern cities:

The enervating life in the cities naturally creates the contrasting relationship from which the open-air movement derives its nourishment, but it is in essence a revival of our animal destiny, a support of a new zest for life, with no regard for whether one directs one's exploring eye at wild nature or the shopping street, which is after all only an intense piece of nature, too. (Jensen 1907: 235)

With this outlook on life, it can hardly surprise anyone to learn that Jensen regarded Theodore Roosevelt as one of his heroes in real life. He was not just an extrovert type; he was also a famous boxer. The key word for him was extroversion. In *Hjulet* ("The Wheel", 1905) the hero Ralf W. Lee ends up defeating his morbid and perverse opponent Evanston in a dramatic boxing match in which he gives Evanston a terrible drubbing. Another of Jensen's heroes from real life is the machine, which is characterized by its combination of harnessed power and energy.

Even in the early novel *Einar Elkær* (1898), which was one of the youthful novels that he later repudiated because of their decadence and degeneration, he invokes the body and physical strength. He says, "We eventually realize that all opinions are wrong, we discover that there is no other poetry than that of the body" (Jensen 1898: 148). It is the facticity of the body that fascinates him, as expressed, for instance, in the poem *Slagsang for Danske Studenters Roklub* ("Battle Song of the Danish Students' Rowing Club"), which praises vigorous joy of life and physical health not only in its content, but also through its form: the poem has a preponderance of nouns, exclamation marks, and follows a strict rhyme and rhythm scheme (Jensen 1954: 51 f.).

A bodily democracy?

Johannes V. Jensen was part of the young democratic – British-inspired – Denmark. It is also striking, however, that he paid scarcely any attention to party-political discussions. For him the actual implementation of democracy was not decisive. For him freedom was primarily synonymous with having an opportunity of influence rather than the degree of influence actually exerted. Correspondingly, equality was more valuable to him as a precondition than as an aim – just as the sprinters in a 100-metre race are differentiated by starting from the same point and running towards the same finishing line.

As part of the new Denmark, Johannes V. Jensen wanted to create a democratic, classless society, but not a society without differences. He and like-minded people strove to liberate the individual by giving him a chance to break free from the system of social classes and groups, so that he had equal opportunity to develop. Yet this potential, according to Jensen, did not mean equality in a social sense as a result. Instead he was thinking about the chance to realize one's bodily, biological powers. Personal development was to be based on physical capacity rather than on the quality of social life. He emphasized the genetic heritage above the social heritage, and he pointed out how important it was for every person to apply himself to using his biological powers as a potential to be realized – with biological differentiation as a result. The ideal was not social but corporeal stratification. Or to put it in another way: what he strove for was a biologistic democracy of opportunity, a bodily democracy. In *Den ny Verden* (1907) he wrote:

> *The solution to the dismal problem of the proletariat in the cities, and for that matter in the countryside too, is to be found in the open-air movement, which alongside the abused wage claims reintroduces the concept of being content with one's lot.* (Jensen 1907: 247).

Here he came seriously close to politics and to the mass culture that was emerging as a social phenomenon. Yet, also here the characteristic Jensenian ideas came out. In *Introduktion til vor Tidsalder* ("Introduction to our Age", 1915) he touched on a delicate topic: the Great War. Obsessed by the relation between the individual and the collective as he was, he mentions both the idea of the English tradition of individual independence and the corresponding perception of Germany's "state discipline" and declares that in modern society we must solve the problem managed long ago by animal organisms, namely, to "bring a multitude of units into a community and a division of labour" (Jensen 1915: 319) since the goal is liberation from the impediments that the individual himself cannot conquer. The ideal state is thus neither individuals running amok nor individuals incapacitated under the yoke of community, but to create a framework in which the assembled powers of the collective allow the individual to develop, instead of using up valuable strength merely to survive. It would be wrong to reduce Johannes V. Jensen to a simple Darwinist. He rather advocated a Nordic version of social liberalism.

Johannes V. Jensen was less worried than many others about the tendency towards the autonomy of the body, which began to appear around the turn of the century and subsequently developed so that bodily culture in the form of sports gradually became a valid sphere of society in its own right. This applied not only in Denmark, but everywhere in Scandinavia. In Sweden we may mention two such different figures as Carl Svedelius, headmaster of Latinskolan Norra Real in Stockholm, who represented the young corporeal century with his propaganda for sports and outdoor life as a counter to anaemic book-learning (Sörlin 1995), and the Social Democratic leader Hjalmar Branting, who unlike many of his party comrades soon realized how sport could be a way to show that the working class, when the terms were equal, could certainly acquit themselves well in competition with the bourgeoisie (Lindroth 1974: 275 ff.).

In Finland the fencing master at Helsinki University, Artur Eklund, was one of the leading theorists of sport and one of those who early understood the special meaning of sport as a gospel of action for young people. But he was also – like Johannes V. Jensen – the one who stressed the quest for harmony as a correlate to pure enthusiasm, and the one who criticized the labour movement for undervaluing the educational and democratic function of sport (Eklund 1970: 81).

"Tordenkalven" and handball

If Johannes V. Jensen is to be singled out as a writer who clearly captured the social climate and the collective mentality in the years around 1900, it is not least of all because we see in him an awareness that movement is not enough. If it is to be able to accomplish anything, this movement must be kept in check. It has to be shaped. Without the constraint of form, it risks being just activism, with vehemence and brute force as the only decisive factors. The physical and sensuous must be flanked by consideration and thought. The ideal is the combination of closeness and distance, self-oblivion and reflection, being present and simultaneously able to view everything from above, as shown in the portrait of one of his prime heroes: "Tordenkalven" (i.e. Thunder Calf), the physically handicapped pedlar from Himmerland, who, precisely, because he was prevented from indulging in many of the physical pleasures of life, was able to portray sensuality with all the greater pregnancy. It was said of him that "he was the most omniscient hedonist that ever described gluttony with a dry mouth" (Jensen 1995: 221). What made him a master was the combination of sensuality and reflection, energy, and measured distance.

In the world of sport, other masters would achieve success, precisely by suspending the desire to rush blindly forward, but not giving up resolute action. The world of sport around 1900 likewise seemed to unite presence and absence – absence in the sense of contemplation, reflection, and a broad perspective. Here, too, the pure lines of the rule system were the necessary frame around the strength and the enthusiasm, ensuring that this did not gain the upper hand. As Johannes V. Jensen writes in *Introduktion til vor Tidsalder*, it is necessary to shape the mass if one wants to move it (Jensen 1915: 318).

It was into this conceptual universe that handball was born around 1900: the desire for order and harmony was to be satisfied while retaining the vitalism and go. Holger Nielsen's own explanation of how he got the idea for the game is illustrative. In the sports publication *Idrætsbogen*, he said that it came about fairly "naturally": he had for some time observed how the boys played with a football before they actually started playing football, and he had noticed that they often used their hands in their eagerness to take possession of the ball. They played in an unstructured, random way, with sudden impulses, steered only by the individual's inclinations and energy. They lacked a framework, a set of rules to ensure that all had the same terms for expressing their will. The relation between individual and collective requires coordination, and so, writes Holger Nielsen, "I had the idea of trying to plan a ball game in which only hands, arms, and head could be used to move the ball" (Nielsen 1909: 145). This is like an echo of Johannes V. Jensen, who in 1898 sketched the utopia of "the agile boy" who could "make a whole of all the pieces". The fragmentary requires form and organization. One cannot rely solely on nature and its spontaneity; it has to be systematized and planned. As he wrote in *Einar Elkær*: "We have long been able to keep time to the music, but now I believe that we should try conducting it" (Jensen 1898: 151).

It was thoughts like these that from 1897 resulted in the game of handball, which would later spread triumphantly over much of the world. It was set in a fixed framework in a society that needed it for an understanding and interpretation of the relation between individual and society at a time when new paths were needed. The old ones were no longer good enough. Handball is in large measure a child of the transition from the nineteenth-century *fin de siècle* to the early twentieth-century cult of youth, movement, and form.

The establishment of handball was by no means unique. The time around 1900 was the period when modern sport was not only introduced but also given a fixed form. Football was organized in national associations in 1889 in both Denmark and Holland. The same happened – thanks to English influence – in New Zealand in 1891, in South Africa and Singapore in 1892, in Argentina in 1893, in Belgium, Switzerland, and Chile in 1895, and in Italy in 1898 (Duke and Crolley 1996: 11). The Olympic Games were revitalized in 1896, the same year as the foundation of the Danish Sports Federation, and also the year that saw the first appearance of two periodicals, *Dansk Sundhedstidende* and *Husmoderens Blad*, and the opening of the Sorø School of Domestic Science, all of which were dedicated to health. The following year, in 1897, the magazine *Ungdom and Idræt* ("Youth and Sport"), published by the Danish Shooting and Gymnastics Associations, began to appear. There was growth everywhere in the Danish health and sports movement in these years.

In 1929 Axel Garde, in an article about Johannes V. Jensen as a lyric poet, wrote about the machine:

> *In its combination of resistant bodies which are so arranged that natural mechanical forces are forced to work in predetermined movements, the machine is a paradigm… It gives us an impression of beauty which corresponds to our sense of movement and balance.*
> (Garde 1989: 30)

Something similar can justifiably be said about a team sport. And it was said. In the sports book *Idrætsbogen*, edited by A.C. Meyer at the start of the century, a centre half is described as "the team's crank, about which the whole machinery turns" (Winding 1909: 43). An age which loved a machine like the bicycle for its harnessed and regulated power obviously had to have a certain weakness for team sports, too. Not because team sports and sportsmen are more machine-like than others, or because the sport is a direct reflection of industrial society and its machinery. One must be aware of any such analogies. It is rather that both team sports and machines are reflections of the social climate in a specific period, Denmark around 1900. It was fairly natural that a historical era like this should "invent" handball. When else could it have happened? The fact that it was invented at the same time in two different places in Denmark, by Holger Nielsen in Copenhagen and by Rasmus Nicolai Ernst in Nyborg in Fyn – in other words, independently by two people – clearly shows that the spirit of the time played a role. In the world of sport, as elsewhere, the right people have to be in the right place at the right time, in relation to what, for want of a better term, we call the *Zeitgeist*.

PAINTING THE NEW BODY: FOUR NORDIC ARTISTS 1900-1914

It is scarcely by chance that fascination with the body at the start of the 20th century also found expression in painting. Everywhere in Scandinavia there are numerous examples of how artists and scholars were preoccupied with the human body, its capacity and vitality; this included pictorial artists. They have always been interested in this, of course, but the special feature of this phase in the history of painting is the particular emphasis on the naked human body. While painters have always painted nudes, the crucial thing now was that the naked human body was painted in dynamic movement in outdoor settings, with neither religion nor eroticism dominating. In other words, it is the body as a body and the joy of movement for its own sake that is prominent. The most pronounced expression of this is in the form of depictions of the naked man's or boy's body in sport and outdoor life, often in connection with scenes of water and bathing.

But perhaps the crucial thing is not the interest in this as a motif in a literary sense: a wish to paint sporting and moving bodies because they are new and interesting. Perhaps it is rather technical painterly problems that are of interest, problems that can be solved with the body as a more or less accidental motif. It is at least obvious that a large number of painters in the first couple of decades of the twentieth century were preoccupied with the relation between, on the one hand, the plastic values of the picture, that is, the spatial structure with character drawing, figure, and background, and on the other hand problems of colour, including problems of value and the effect of light on the character of colour. For this, pictures of bodies in outdoor lighting, *plein-air* paintings with horizon and sunlight, offered a possibility.

Yet the next questions arise at once: Why bodies to solve these painterly problems? Was it the artistic challenge that was at stake? Or was it the desire for ethnological representations of popular life? These questions call for an answer when, for example, one looks at the Danish art painter Jens Søndergaard's pictures of folk life. Søndergaard loved tilting at the ring, animal shows, and gymnastic contests, but as regards his painting, these seem more like an excuse. In a series of letters to Poul Uttenreiter from the early 1950s he writes of how he looked forward to these festivities, but he gives no specific information about why they fascinated him – apart from the fact that he took along "a whole crate of beer and a bottle of djin etc." as provisions, so that he could see better (cited here from Zahle 1994: 78). The painterly aspect is so self-evident that he does not bother to mention it.

And here we have his paintings to fall back on. They show that it is the rhythm and repetition in a dynamized space, combined with the small shades of almost-similarity that concerns him, that is, the nuances. And of course he always paints these dynamic bodies in a landscape. It is hardly an accident, because it gives him the opportunity to localize the activities. They are not placed in an abstract vacuum. The bodies are a bastion against the abstraction and academic speculation that Søndergaard could never tolerate, never got involved in, and never managed to understand.

The result is a triad consisting of the dual gaze of the painter – for the independent logic of the picture and the structures of the movement motif – in interplay with the landscape as the third factor. Here the down-to-earth connection with the landscape helps to maintain the balance. Too much pictorial logic gives too great a character of style, taste, and firm grasp, easily leading to dryness of content and style for its own sake, concerned only with the precious and the decorative, while, the reverse – too much mere rendering of the motif – involves the risk of illustration of concepts and ideas, so that one fails the pictorial aspect and contents oneself with rendering and reflecting.

Søndergaard solves this problem in a refined way, by searching out motifs which in themselves contain pictorial potential: water, beach, and body. Here he can let his paintings unfold in the tension between the local and the universal, between empirical and cosmic, between primitivism and refinement, as was said about one of his kindred spirits, the Finnish painter Gallén-Kallela (Laugesen 1992: 22). But other painters before him had done this, all over Scandinavia in the time up to the First World War.

It is this interest in the human body performing sport and in the open air that we shall look at. How is the human body portrayed? What perception of the body lies behind it? What is it that fascinates? These are some of the questions to be answered in this article. This is done on the basis of the view that perception of body and space alike in this period underwent a transformation and witnessed a shift – and that this shift can be found in all the Nordic countries, with similarities and differences. There will thus be an emphasis on a comparative examination of the phenomenon.

Bodily aristocrats of everyday life

In this connection it is interesting to see what these contemporary painters fastened upon. One insight into this can be obtained from the observations of the Finland-Swedish architect, art writer, and collector Sigurd Frosterus in his book *Olikartade skönhetsvärden* ("Differing Aesthetic Values") from 1915. The book is a rhapsody of impressions of journeys in Europe, and it contains pieces written back in the first years of the century, when he started considering contemporary foreign art in the culture magazine *Euterpe*, because he had caught a whiff of a new departure in both artistic and spatial terms. One of the places Frosterus describes is Siena. A major point of his is the endeavour to show the relationship between nature and art (in this case architecture), where it was evidently worth trying to achieve a balance between these two entities, as otherwise there is the risk that they end up in a dichotomous opposition.

Yet it is just as clear that Frosterus, in his desire to look at nature when dealing with art, is simultaneously fascinated with a pure artistic order. "Siena should be seen in the winter", he writes:

> while the air is clear and cold and clean, when the contours are firm and hard, as if drawn with coarse ink lines, and the colours, without blurred edges, without transitions, contrast sharply with each other as in glass mosaics set in lead. (Frosterus 1915: 13)

He later uses adjectives like "uniform, severe, stylized". No rural idyll with romance and curved, soft lines here. The ideal cannot be mistaken: "An exuberance of suppleness lies bound within simple walls" (Frosterus 1915: 20).

Controlled power and vitality are the motto of the times, with due consideration for spirit and soul. The style is aristocratic with a sense of non-utilitarian superfluity: ornament and sport for pure fun go nicely hand in hand here, as when he writes enthusiastically about lawn tennis as a noble sport, and as an activity that "our plebeian time" has little feeling for. He is impressed by the world champion, A.F. Wilding, who plays tennis as he plays billiards:

> *Seemingly slow, carefully calculated and considered movements. No nervous haste, no vigorous zeal. Nothing for empty effect. When he kills a ball he does with playful ease, as if it were the only natural thing, the only possible thing.* (Frosterus 1915: 286)

Once again: control and a sense of what is appropriate in relation to the actual sporting-artistic act, and just as much a rejection of empty splendour on the one hand and insistent pragmatism and bourgeois common sense about busy everyday tasks on the other hand. Frosterus hits out violently at the medieval towns of Germany, whose inhabitants, in his eyes, have always been suppressed under the yoke of the guild system and shrewd pragmatism (Frosterus 1915: 27).

It is the self-aware individual speaking here, with a spiritual and bodily aristocracy, elevated above humdrum everyday triviality, longing for a purer, more magnificent world. He speaks of an extraordinary universe, where the social is in the shadow of the artistic and the cultural. He seeks a world where beauty – understood as a combination of a fixed backdrop and movement for its own sake – has pride of place. No wonder he quotes elsewhere in the book the "Midnight Song" from Nietzsche's *Zarathustra*, which was so popular at the time:

> *Die Welt is tief*
> *und tiefer als der Tag gedacht*

This passage is about the excess that is *of* this world but not *in* it. It inspired many artists, painters and writers, who used it as a fulcrum in their desire to cope with and disregard the obvious jumble of everyday pettiness and common sense, while simultaneously wanting to take part in mundane life with its sensuous tasks. Ultimately, the aim was to pump new energy and magnificence into everyday life. It is the banality and lifelessness of everyday life, rather than everyday life itself, that is attacked. They did not want to be content, they also felt a duty. The outlook was probably aristocratic, but the aim, paradoxically, was to make the aristocratic democratic and popular.

In this way Frosterus – who is regarded as one of the precursors of the functionalism and cultural radicalism that lasted longer in Finland than in the other Nordic countries (Kayser Nielsen 1997c) – is also a man of the new, young, optimistic century. In a letter written to his mother in 1904 he writes about the encounter with the big city of Berlin, that he had the feeling that the scales fell from his eyes and that "new values suddenly stepped forward, it was like waking from a dream to a richer and living reality" (quoted from Kasvio 1992: 31).

This had to have artistic consequences as well. In another letter to his mother from 1906 he writes: "The art of the future will teach the method of looking around with wide-awake eyes" (quoted from Kasvio 1992: 32). It is like hearing another great awakener, Johannes V. Jensen, from the same period. He too wanted to look around him with open eyes. He wanted to become wiser.

Thirty years after the publication of *Olikartade skönhetsvärden*, Sigurd Frosterus writes with equal enthusiasm about his kindred spirit Johannes V. Jensen and his fascination with the cycling girls of Copenhagen, incarnated in the office girl Gudrun "as an expression of peaceful evolution: a carefree prosperity just a bit above the hunger line" (Frosterus 1946: 85). On her free-and-easy progress "in the flow of traffic through the street on the way to work and in her spare time to the beach or the beech woods", Gudrun becomes a symbol both of the progress of civilization and of how corporeality comes into its own. She is – as viewed through a lens from before the First World War – an anonymous aristocrat of everyday life.

It is the dream of this aristocratic beauty of body and soul that was crucial for the painters and writers who criticized their own time, who could not be satisfied with just social progress. For them physical improvement was not equated with food on the table; one should also like bathing in sunlight – and be good at tennis.

Edvard Munch and the posing bathers

It is no wonder that Sigurd Frosterus also threw himself upon Edvard Munch and his sensory evangelism and Nietzsche-inspired fascination with the body and the solutions of corporeality to the "sickness unto death" of the West. I am thinking here of Munch's Warnemünde breakthrough in the summer of 1907 when, sick in soul and mind as a result of both persecution mania and excessive alcohol consumption, he sought consolation in Nietzsche's words from *Zarathustra* about how, instead of listening to oneself, one should listen to one's body (at that time it was not an inflated cliché). He therefore painted vital, naked men, yellow from the colour of the sun and red in the face, rising from the blue and green sea with broad strides.

Frosterus mentions this as a turning point in Munch's art; his endeavour is to free himself from the maelstrom of self-absorption. Munch becomes a sun worshipper, and the dissonances dissolve into cooler, more harmonious chords, according to Frosterus (1916: 39). Ragna Stang is thinking on the same lines when she claims that Munch here wanted to work his way out of the straitjacket of self-centredness. He wanted to be as vital as the strong, naked men he painted (Stang 1978: 197).

The pictures of Munch's German period do not reflect what he remembers as an expressionist painter but what he sees. His eyes are wide open, and the introspection is (for a while) suspended. At the same time, this period shows, if any in his life does, that there is no substance in the otherwise traditional view that Munch generally painted his own life, as a gesture of rationalizing after the fact, as introverted and psychologizing painting. We see here, as is claimed by the latest research and exhibition activities concerning Munch, that he also had a wide-awake gaze for contemporary issues of a general cultural character that interested an intellectually and internationally alert artist.

There is of course something to this talk, as one realizes from observing the photograph of Munch on the beach at Warnemünde the same summer. He is shown posing in bold masculine stance, with proudly straddled legs, short bathing trunks, and with brush in hand; with a nude male model in the background and with the painting just behind him. In all its constructed and arranged masculinity, the photograph shows Munch in a transitional situation, where it is difficult to draw the boundary between the artist and the outdoor person. He is making vigorous efforts to put his mental crisis behind him, instead devoting himself to the strong, healthy simplicity of open-air life, in sun-drenched enterprise.

In both the version of the picture *Men Bathing* from 1911, which hangs in the Munch Museum in Oslo, and the 1907 version in the Atheneum in Helsinki, Munch's water aristocrats have their red-shining legs firmly planted on the ground. More specifically, they tread the warm, sunlit beach with self-confidence, rushing vertically, while their heads are flush with the blue sea on the horizon. It is as if they are holding their heads high, but also cold, in the midst of their bold go-ahead spirit. They have vitality and a thirst for life, but with composure and control: Power without running amok. The cold heads give the men a certain cool and cynically overbearing character. They do not seem kind and sociable, these men.

Their dark faces, one of them bearded, are paralleled by the crotches, where the hair cover is depicted, as are the male organs. Yet these are not brute males that are portrayed, but civilized masculine worshippers of life in simple nakedness, but the sex indicates that we are nevertheless in the century of biologism, when the biological had to be united with the social. At this point the word *social* was used to denote history and the social sciences and – gradually – also biology (Liedman 1997: 53 ff.). At the same time, however, the ideal is clearly not the naked person but the adult, naked man who conquers life. It is thus a culturalized naked person.

Contemporaries reacted violently to this unveiled portrait of Munch's self-aware, loose-limbed men. In the autumn of 1907 the Clematis art gallery refused to exhibit the painting, since it was feared that such a direct tribute to manhood would be reported to the police (Eggum 1983: 217).

In 1918, however, Munch took up the theme once again in the painting *Man Bathing*. This time it is less of an apotheosis of the naked male body. It is more a case of the incorporation of humans in nature, with the sunlit muscles of the men's bodies reflected in and reflecting the light and water. The circular lines of the male body, almost anticipating cubism, have their counterpart in the line of the rock in the background and the stones on the beach in the foreground.

There is vitalism here because it is not connected to that of the body itself but to the general physical effect, less powerful and strained and softer than in the previous bathing pictures. At the same time, the purely painterly aspects have become more important than the intention and the ideology. The proclamatory devil-may-care attitude has been toned down in favour of an exploration of problems of colour. Unfortunately, this has been done at the expense of quality.

The first bathing pictures – despite their lack of orientation to the technical aspects of painting – are none the less better and more rounded paintings. With their bright and raw colours they are fresher and healthier in all their boldness. The rather staged combination of outdoor person and artist had its advantages, perhaps because it so evidently, but also innovatively, centred around the marked and acknowledged artistry. Yet these pictures had their weaknesses, too. The weakness is that it is groomed: the picture is willed. Munch has listened too much to the Zeitgeist. He has produced a picture that is fine as a painting, but it reeks of intentionality in the midst of the technical achievement. The balance does not succeed. The productive tension, which otherwise always gives Munch's paintings their power, is degraded here to unctuous fidelity to the spirit of the age – despite all his defiance: he wants too much here.

Magnus Enckell and pure colours

Munch was not the only one who painted beaches and naked people in those years. Above I held up Sigurd Frosterus as a catalyst of a new, sunlit view of reality in the Finnish art debate. Frosterus also tried his hand at some nude beach watercolours from the Lido in Italy, when he was on holiday there in spring 1906, but mostly out of lip service. "I do it for my own pleasure, to sharpen my eye", he wrote home.

The person who implemented Frosterus' programme in painterly terms was instead Magnus Enckell. By 1908 he had already painted a series of pictures of light and air, some in oil, some in watercolour, from the harbour in Helsinki, with a blindingly sharp and cold light against the waterfront. With the blue sky as a contrast, the pictures radiate a chilly, controlled sensual joy. The pictures are clearly influenced by impressionism, yet at the same time they contain a distinctive Nordic melancholy which relativizes the purely technical skill that otherwise impresses with its delicate mastery of colour and a strict organization of the pictorial potential of the motif. At the same time, the pictures are "true": Anyone who has experienced both the spring light and the liquor-sharp autumn air of Helsinki knows that Enckell does not offend against realism in the midst of the artistic display. A dozen years later the impressionistic spring delicacy is replaced by more luxuriant and romantic, expressionistically influenced paintings. Enckell's colour scale has become darker.

Between these two periods lies a transition phase, and like Munch, Magnus Enckell paints naked people on the beach in his transition. This takes place in the period that is regarded as the most brilliant ever in Finnish painting, namely, the years 1910-1920. In these years Enckell painted his open-air pictures of naked people on the border between land and water, including the painting *Boys on the Beach* and the little sketch *From Hogland*, which are perhaps Enckell's very best from those years. Here on the island in the middle of the Gulf of Finland, Enckell retains the lyrical delicacy from the harbour motifs of a few years previously, while displaying a freshness and a vital sensuality which he never subsequently managed to surpass. The sunlight beats down over the shore and into the observer. It is a raw vitalism – exposed to cosmic overtones and nature-evangelism – with people who are quite simply happy to be alive. At the same time, *Boys on the Beach* in particular anticipates his expressionist, heavier colour scale. Blue, pink, purple, green, red, and yellow, with one of the boys' bright red, while the other has a bluish-green torso in the faint reflection of the light, while his face and legs are coloured red.

The most characteristic feature, however, is the purity of the colours. The picture is more painterly than literary. The vitalism is obvious enough, but it is based on artistic problems. It is of course telling us about the pleasure of the open air and boyish dynamism, but it is first and foremost the effort to avoid colour transitions and to show off the pure pallet that strikes us. The colours are stretched close up against each other in an unmixed spectrum. Pure, shining colour tone is the goal but also – of course – the means, when the motif is plucky boys, rock-hard cliffs, and blinding late summer light in the afternoon, when the shadows grow long. And:

Perhaps it is precisely because Enckell is so indifferent to the literary, in other words, that he does not care about the intentional, that he is able to depict vitality: he forgets the words and grammar and concentrates more on the language of experience than that of knowledge.

The mental reverberation and self-analytical posing that characterizes Munch's paintings from the same year is totally absent in Enckell. Here it is body and untroubled boyish pranks rather than hard-won manhood. Enckell's boys seem to have eaten rye bread all their carefree days, while Munch and his men seem just to have started to do so. As Jacob Paludan writes about Thomas Mann's little novel *Tonio Kröger*, with scenes from bathing life and Tonio's falling in love with the doctor's fair-haired daughter, Inge Holm:

> *It enchants, as the gaze of a stranger on our over-described localities can do, it has a heartbeat that is not common in the analysing author. Let me look into it when nausea caused by too many printed things feels as if it is just around the corner. It has the breeze, September light, C Major.* (Paludan s. a.: 5f.)

The same applies to Enckell's bathing boys. They, too, are liberated from the eternal problems of the time and of humanity. One cannot even say that they enjoy life; they simply are life – placed in a space between the local and the cosmic, they are in their element, or as the Germans say, *in seinem Esse*, which comes from the Latin verb meaning "to be".

J.F. Willumsen, meaning and cosmos

In Enckell the cosmic is toned down in favour of sheer healthiness of movement and self-expression. In Willumsen the reverse is true, and even more so as the years passed. Whereas Enckell left behind the beach-loving children and the naked bodies, Willumsen nourished a lifelong interest in this, although the naked people from his later works have a more symbolic and perhaps deep psychological meaning (Buurgaard 1997). I therefore ignore them here.

Instead we shall look more closely at the bathing pictures that Willumsen produced in the same period as the other artists we have considered here, that is, in the years between 1900 and 1914. Here alone there is enough to seize on. Willumsen shared the great contemporary interest in the body, but he did so in his own dynamic fashion. For him the painting is more important than the motif. The body and its movement interest him above all as form: "The main thing is the *bending* of the body, the limbs, and the fingers. The tilting of the head, the character of the musculature" (Krogh 1987: 22), as he wrote on 15 January 1899 to Alice Bloch, a friend who was interested in art, formerly married to the art historian Emil Hannover.

Thanks to the letters to her we also have an opportunity to look more closely at Willumsen as regards his portraits of bathing children. He began his studies for this in 1902, when he was in Amalfi together with his lover and later his wife, Edith. He cannot stand being there. The Italians are riff-raff, he writes home:

> *There can scarcely be worse rabble, swine, swindlers on this earth. It is impossible to stay any length of time here. This is a people on the lowest level. Three hundred years ago there was a time of prosperity with a sense of beauty. The great palaces with the coats of arms on the entry arch are now occupied by rabble, making a mess and cackling, with no capacity even to maintain what they have inherited from their forefathers. They behave like dogs and answer the call of nature on stairs and in the middle of the street. In broad daylight. They are degenerate in every way…* (Krogh 1987: 28 f.)

It is thus neither the noble savage nor the picturesque exotic that Willumsen sees in southern Italy. His business is neither salon art with *osterìa* scenes nor kitschy pictures of Danish artists' colonies. He is looking for the many forms and expressions of the naked human body. And perhaps not even the forms and movements of the body, but rather all the different forms and movements that can be produced at all, but in this case by a body. The Italians boys are paid to pose on the beach: 10 øre to stand on one leg and hold the sock on the other while Willumsen takes a photograph (Krogh 1995: 81 ff.). The result was a series of photographs taken in 1902 and in 1904, when Willumsen returned. That same year, in August, he went on to the south coast of Brittany, because the sea and the beach in south Italy could not satisfy his desire to capture the rhythmic series of long, rolling waves on a wide, bare beach. Willumsen went about things systematically in his thirst for knowledge about the agreement of form and expression.

The result of his efforts came already in 1904, when he made a series of sketches in oils with the title *Bathing Children*. The final result, however, was not to come until a few years later, in the shape of the large picture entitled *Bathing Children on the Beach at Skagen*, on which he worked in the summer of 1909, the final version with the title *Sun and Youth: Children on the Beach* from 1910, which today adorns the end wall in one of the galleries in the Göteborg Museum of Art. In relation to the original from 1904 it is plain to see that there has been a shift away from the maritime towards the combination of people and sea. In the 1904 version, although one can see four or five bathing figures out in the sea, it is mostly a seascape. This is very different from the two almost identical versions from 1909 and 1910. Here we are much closer to the sea and to the people.

In compositional terms the picture is built up of the contrast between, on the one hand, the infinity of the sea and the shoreline, as regards both length and breadth, and on the other hand the nearness in the form of the many children on their way out into the water. As he had pointed out in 1899 in the letter to Alice Bloch cited above, it is the harmony between the whole and the details that is crucial. In *Sun and Youth* this duality consists of the "always" of the sea and the water and the "now" of the bathing. At the same time, each of the children is captured in a different phase of a rhythmic course of events. Like Jens Søndergaard later in his pictures of men tilting at the ring, the artist is interested in the unique and distinctive form of the suppleness and of every single phase of the movement as part of a concerted movement. Willumsen here is a kind of movement analyst – but an artistic one, for he is less concerned with the purely biological and clinical gaze than with the total movement, which he then dissects with an analytic intent, to investigate its purely painterly potential. The fact that pride of place is given to the painterly qualities is obvious from his laborious work between the contrast effect in the form of the distribution of light and shade on the children's bodies and on the surface of the water and the sand.

More than in any of his contemporaries, it is the human body placed in a space that concerns him, with the final character of the body and its capacity to create unique moments being contrasted with the rhythmic waves of the sea with its eternally repeated movement. *Sun and Youth* has the character of a nature scene, but as always with Willumsen, this nature is peopled. In other words, the searchlight is pointed at the ability of the human body to set its stamp on nature and its ability – via contrast – to let nature come into its own. In the final analysis, this is a refined way of playing with and exploring the heartfelt cultural question of the creation of meaning in the relationship between difference and similarity. Willumsen is not a dreamy romantic, he is an art painter. In him more than anyone else, we see the tension between the body as an occasion for creating art and the delight in the body's own dexterity. Here the tension between the motif and the painterly aspect is stretched as tight as it could be at that time.

By virtue of this interest in meaning and its preconditions, it is scarcely surprising that Willumsen also had to feel an almost panic fear of the nature that just exists in all its cosmological dumbness and impenetrable silence. This "meaninglessness" of nature is symbolized in his works by the sun as the all-devouring and consuming power, which crushes people with its wordless cruelty, as we see thematized in *After the Storm* from 1905 and even worse in the gruesome painting in oil and tempera from 1916 entitled *Fear of Nature: After the Storm 2*. It is in the starkest possible contrast to the balance of nature and culture, of difference and similarity, which is expressed in the bathing pictures from the first decade of the century, and to that expressed in *A Female Mountaineer* from 1914. Here the dichotomy is not deadly but productive.

Willumsen was reproached by contemporaries who thought that *Sun and Youth* lacked atmosphere. The artist replied on this point that his intention was not to paint atmospheres, if by that one understood something vague and moribund, in "half-light", that is, an evening mood: "Why is there no such thing as day mood? Don't the radiant sun, the fresh sea, and the naked children also have a mood about them?" he asked rhetorically (Moltesen 1923: 28). For him, clarity of form and bright colours as a way to render light and vitality gave just as legitimate a mood as the melancholy of *fin de siècle* painting in the 1890s.

Eugène Jansson going sportive

While the painters we have hitherto dealt with have painted outdoor physical activities, this has not been in the service of sport in the strict sense, but more with the character of outdoor life. This is not the case with the Swedish painter Eugène Jansson, however. His works bring us indoors to look at true sporting activity. It may seem strange at first sight, that Jansson – in his earlier artistic practice – was also the most melancholic and lyrical of all the painters here. Not for no reason was he called "the painter of the blue city", since his earlier works were painted in the elegiac style of the 1890s, as represented and promoted by the Swedish Prince Eugen and others. These two painters were so close, the king's son and the poor orphan from the working-class districts of Södermalm, that their artist friends called Eugène Jansson *Fotogen* ("Paraffin", rhyming with Eugène/Eugen) to distinguish them. Another reason was that Jansson diluted his paints with paraffin and turpentine (Zachau 1998: 37).

The elegiac paintings with their bewitching blue colouring and a long series of views over the blue waters of Stockholm were linked to the national romantic painting that flourished in the 1890s in Sweden. This cultivated melancholy, often with motifs of evening and night. It is a twilight painting with dark pastels and blurred outlines, aimed at rendering moods, where the observer's gaze is supposed to be led deeper and deeper into the blue mystique of the painting. As Henrik Cornell points out in his book about the history of Swedish art, the important thing for Jansson in this phase of his artistic progress is to distance himself from what is close in time and place (Cornell 1959: 222). For that reason the foreground in his pictures is normally empty. This is the world from which we long to get away, into the symbolically hinted distant horizon. We see a romanticized, "deep" painting with an aestheticizing attitude to life, which belongs in the dream world of art. Perhaps it has also been coloured by Jansson's own frailty as a child (like Munch) and his extremely poor living conditions as a young man.

And then came the breakthrough; in the years around 1905, to be precise. He changed both his colours and his circle of motifs. This hardly happened by chance. For one thing, he was influenced by the contemporary enthusiasm for sport; for another, it was a consequence of his own interest in athletics and physical exercises (Zachau 1998: 40). Ever since he had contracted scarlet fever as a 13-year-old, he had used sport as part of a tough regime of physical rehabilitation, training so hard that at times it almost cost him his life. In other words, it was a pronounced body connoisseur who now stepped into character. He did so with full strength. It was probably in 1906 (the dating is uncertain) that he painted his first naked study: a young man, well-built with a tattoo on his lower left arm. There are no cosmic overtones here, no gospel of fresh air.

In its wealth of realistic detail, the painting is almost like an illustration from a medical book. It is an extremely sober and far from romantic painting that meets the observer. The only testimony to the past is that Jansson's fondness for the gloomy colours of twilight still dominates. Otherwise, the picture is characterized by a striking lack of illusion. The only thing we are supposed to see is a naked man's body: Neither more nor less.

The next year he painted perhaps his most famous painting from his vitalistic second period: the big (roughly 2 × 3 m) painting entitled *The Navy Bath-House*. Now sport enters the picture. And here the foreground is completely filled; the here-and-now of reality makes itself palpable. The painting is dominated by sunlit, well-built youths, all directing their attention towards the central motif, the diver, hovering like an arrow above the water in the pool, in a sportingly correct style study. As a backdrop he has the blue sky and the group of greenish-blue trees that cut across the border between the water and the air. In the background there is a crowd of admiring spectators. In compositional terms the painting is built up of powerful horizontal and vertical lines, effectively using the potential of the bath-house landscape, in the form of water lines and the wooden pillars of the pavilions, to provide a frame for a parallelogram of forces. As regards colour, the artist operates with a similar contrast between the strong, hot sun and the blue chilliness of water and sky. Life here is not elegiac, but dynamic and full of tension. Jansson depicts it as tough, in a craftsmanlike and sober way.

In the following year, he once again tackled the bath-house motif, in the painting *Bathing Picture*. Here the perspective has been turned half-way. This time we see the diver from the back instead of from the side. Yet, he still hovers above the water, this time like something in-between a bird and an aeroplane. He is still the concentrated centre point to which everyone directs their gaze; and here, too, in the foreground we see the muscular young men with washboard stomachs, sexual organs, and powerful shoulders. And this time more in harmony with the textbook of human biology than with a nature gospel.

Yet another later picture follows in 1911: *Bath-House*. Here we are down at the level of the water and see the naked swimmers, yellowish-white against the blue of the water. Sweden's national colours, but without any direct allusion to the national romantic project. The patriotism of the Oscarian era – Sweden's counterpart to the Victorian period – with its mixture of melancholy and grand gestures, is succeeded here by a new tendency to freshness and daring. "Sweden" is now not so much in the thoughts as in the movements, that is, more in the body than in the soul. We have finally entered the twentieth century, albeit still sticking somewhat to tradition. The lines still consist of right angles with a tension between horizontal and vertical lines, between low water level and robust ascent.

From 1912 comes a change of motif. Jansson moves indoors and paints acrobats, wrestlers, and weightlifters. Aquatic agility is replaced by the cultivation of strength, with a keen interest in the compositional possibilities in the parallelism of bodies. The two wrestlers are both pressing heavily against each other, in the same way as the acrobats do, with one on the floor and the other in the air; their arms and torsos repeating each other in mirror image. It is the capacity of the bodies for combination and harmony that is now in the centre, while the loner in the shape of the weightlifter still makes himself felt. Jansson was always a man of continuity even in the midst of all his innovative thinking.

The fact that all this has a more or less acknowledged connection with homosexuality (as the gossip at the time hinted) is irrelevant in this context. What tempts Jansson is the joy of being able to paint the strength and competence of the human body. In this way he anticipates the sporting breakthrough that took place in the same year – 1912 – as the Olympic Games were held in Stockholm: in blazing sun. It was called the "Sunshine Olympics". Jansson may have approved of the epithet, but we know nothing about that. Here

again, words are not enough. Luckily, however, the paintings say a
great deal. They anticipate what would come to full development
– for better or worse – in the interwar years; at the same time, it
completes what had been on the way ever since Bruno Liljefors's
paintings from the 1880s.

Body culture and Zeitgeist

The famous painter of animals and nature, Bruno Liljefors, had
already started in the 1880s to tackle the triad of nature, art, and
sport. With his well-trained body he was able to pose as a model
for the other pupils at the school of theory of the Royal Academy
of Fine Arts in Stockholm (Ellenius 1997: 52). He produced numerous illustrations for contemporary sports literature, and at the same
time he engaged in athletics himself. He was particularly interested
in boxing and gymnastics, and performed daily gymnastics until an
advanced age. He had parallel bars standing in his studio (Örsan
1994: 132).

Liljefors, however, never really formed a school. Only a few
Nordic artists followed in his footsteps. Harald Giersing's famous
painting *Fodboldspillere. Sofus header* is one example, Jens Søndergaard's painting of a football match in Thy is another. One of the
most recent manifestations was the exhibition entitled *Sport in Art*
arranged in the Art Gallery in Göteborg in 1995, when the World
Athletic Championships were held there. As a whole, art and sport
have gone separate ways.

As we have seen, however, there are occasional artists who have
taken an interest in the dynamics of sport, play, and outdoor life.
Among them are the four selected here, whose common denominator
is that they produced their most famous paintings of bodies in the
period between the late nineteenth-century mood of melancholy
decadence and the vigorous optimism of the early twentieth century,
that is, the period when sport really caught on. This link between
nature, art, and sport did not happen overnight; it was rather a case
of a protracted evolutionary course. Another common feature is
that the sports pictures, even in the artists' own life histories, mark
a transition from crisis and depression to love of life and renewed
strength.

It can be difficult to gain a definitive understanding of what features of sport fascinated the artists. Yet we may perhaps find an explanation in Bruno Liljefors, when he points out the relationship between peace and stillness on the one hand, gliding into speed, dynamism, and bold action on the other:

> *What I relish in the flying trapeze is the long, logical harmony that is achieved, following consistently into the boldest positions, through the perfection of the bodies and the imperturbable precision of the acrobat in the game he can afford to play.* (Cited from Ellenius 1997: 54)

Liljefors is not alone in this view, which in its own way – in the movement's own tacit knowledge – perhaps also illustrates and interprets the transition between the quiet 1890s and the lively years between 1900 and 1914. August Nitschke, historian of the body, is perhaps thinking along the same lines in his book *Körper in Bewegung*, when he mentions the great interest of the period in movements connecting two poles, for example, the contrast between breathing in and breathing out, raising and lowering, and so on (Nitschke 1989: 325). In other words, it looks as if both sport and painting are part of a unified collective mentality in the tension-filled era between decline and flourishing that characterized these years.

The body in shape

When one looks at Jansson's pictures it is often difficult to avoid having the impression that something new has finally caught on. It is no longer demonstrative presentations of the naked, healthy male body that are interesting, as with Edvard Munch; nor is it the cheerful beach boys as with Magnus Enckell, who are just happy to be alive. It is also far from Willumsen's pathetic, cosmically oriented horror of nature and his semiotic interest in meaning and its formation. Jansson is less pathetic than Munch and Willumsen, but also more pledged to the motifs than Enckell. He is a representative of the essence of sport. The power is now systematized and shaped much less in a Nietzschean and martial way than in the muscular attitude that radiated from Munch's naked bathing men. At the same time, it is clear that the cheerful element of play that characterizes Enckell's "water dogs", here where we are dealing with sport, is organized and regulated with codes and controlled achievements. In this way the painters around 1910 also contribute to the encircling of the bodily development that would be witnessed in the course of the twentieth century: sport between dead earnest and carefree play, between vitalistic superman-ism and relational, peaceful bodily cooperation.

There are thus considerable differences between the four perceptions of the body and its essence. At the same time, there is also a fundamental similarity by virtue of the at once enthusiastic/curious but also fearful/attractive fascination with corporeality and its new appearance on the stage which is so characteristic of the first couple of decades of the twentieth century, when the biological and the artistic grappled with each other.

At the same time, these Nordic painters' presentation and definition of the body, play, sport, and outdoor life may be a reminder that sport is not solely sport and records; it also contains an artistic and visual dimension. It seems to be increasingly forgotten as performance and competition have taken over and turned sport into idiotic commerce. In the first fresh decades of the twentieth century, people were highly aware of the aesthetic dimension – it was a matter of the arousal of both mind and body. Literature, sport, and art contributed in equal measure to presenting the possibilities for bodily education and liberation that were now available, helping to demonstrate a new knowledge about the body and the senses.

THE "SUNSHINE OLYMPICS": STOCKHOLM 1912

It has been called the Sunshine Olympics. It was warm that summer, but there were also other reasons for the name (Rydén 1994). For the Olympic Games in Stockholm in 1912 also heralded a new era: First of all, people were saying goodbye to the disillusioned, *fin-de-siècle* atmosphere and instead began to follow a broad social "Jugendstil" (Bayertz 1990), in which the youth came into focus as the new vital and dynamic generation that defeated the melancholy and weak dandy, who was more interested in style and self-staging than actions and doings. Second, they were abandoning a stiff and closed conception of space and devoting themselves to a new cultivation of space as a field of projection and development; space should first and foremost be a field of expansion and of action, dominated by lines of force and tension curves. Thirdly, they had also defeated the old-fashioned punch patriotism, with its emphasis on national awareness for the select few, paving the way for a new democratic nationalism that praised the general population's physical culture; and, finally, with the Stockholm Olympics it became clear for the first time that physical activities can have a value of their own. This would be a frequently recurring theme up through the twentieth century.

At the end of the nineteenth century, people had a sense that the Western world was on the decline, that they were too late, and that it was evening time. Especially in German intellectual circles, represented among others by Max Nordau and Herbert Spengler, the idea spread that culture was being forced in the background of civilisation with its superficiality and unhealthy decline, where capitalistic egoism and raw working masses set the stage (Kayser Nielsen 1994b). From Germany this idea spread to Scandinavia, where the 1890s were often depicted by moonstruck, remote young men who were afraid of women, nature, the body, and the new times. Edvard Munch's paintings and Johannes Jørgensen's poetry on "erotically deprived violins" on the side streets were typical effects of this fear. This fear of the course of history was linked to a basic pessimism as a result, in particular, of the theory of heredity tied to the mechanical-deterministic view of life prevalent in the Scandinavian countries from the 1880s onward, manifested, for instance, in works like Herman Bang's *Håbløse slægter* (Hopeless relations) and Henrik Ibsen's *Ghosts*.

But change was on the way. Anders Zorn's exuberant "dalakullor" (girls from Dalarna), Johannes V. Jensen's intense confrontation with his own obsession with reflection, and Knut Hamsun's interest in the mystical forces of nature, gender and the body testify to new times. In about 1900 a wave of sun, light, and round-cheeked optimism began spreading across Scandinavia. This took place for one thing under the influence of Germany, where the idea of "youth" had become the new solution – the youth that across class boundaries, particular interests, and unhealthy decline paints a picture of thaw, spring and summer. The biological prevails over the social. Often this faith in the biological-physical condition, condensed in the vitality of youth, is accompanied by the notion of a biological democracy: that people meet and are differentiated by virtue of their physical constitution and capabilities more than their social heritage. This transition from decadent maturity to vitalistic youth is expressed in its most condensed form on Danish soil in the periodical entitled *Vagten*, which L. Mylius-Erichsen published in 1899-1900. The two very first lines in the periodical are significant:

> *It is soon time that an honest goal*
> *shine through the day's futile bawl!*
> (Vagten 1899-1900: 1)

This aim soon became evident in the form of doings and actions as the watchwords of the time more than in the form of a new philosophy or a new religion. The body stood for the goal more than thought and the soul. In the same periodical Axel Garde asks rhetorically – and symptomatically: "Whom does it help, whom does it please when someone stands up and speaks of his soul's dreams and then becomes lost in the tortuous words and finished thoughts of old books" (*Vagten* 1899-1900: 23). The optimistic confidence in the youthful body as the solution to the problem of the times was not least a result of the German discovery of youth, outdoor life, and enthusiasm for life at the end of the nineteenth century. Communicated by Georg Brandes and Ola Hansson, Nietzsche's confrontation with decadence, the spectator mentality, and hostility towards the body manifested itself many places in Scandinavian intellectual life. Not only in literature and philosophy, but also in the shape of a vitalistic art of painting that with a glaring and frank range of colours cultivates the naked body with strong torsos and contours and praises outdoor life and fresh air. Significant for the confrontation with the old and turn toward the new, healthy and vigorous is Anders Zorn's depiction of his first attempt in the genre:

> *I got a (fat) sweet boiler from the Academy, was sailed out to a nearby island by a man from Dalarö, and painted some bathing women there after this buxom girl. A combination of grey cliffs, fir trees, nudity and water.* (Quoted from Brummer 1995: 137 f.)

Several years later, in 1907, Eugène Jansson completed his painting *Flottans badhus*. Previously, Jansson had usually painted in the lyrical style of Prince Eugen of Sweden from the 1890s, but now threw himself into motifs with athletic men surrounded by rays of sunlight. Until 1912 he continued to work in this genre and depicted bodies in various positions. He was not just interested in well-proportioned and perfect bodies, but realistically painted young men with bodies that were just as different as those of the spectators (Zachau 1998: 40). But also within sports circles, Nietzsche found a willing ear, especially in the Finnish-Swedish sports philosopher and writer Artur Eklund, who, like Johannes V. Jensen, was also a great admirer of Theodore Roosevelt. Inspired by Nietzsche, Eklund could among other things write that

> *Sport is the cultivation of physical glory, of action... It may seem materialistically cramped yet it is pervaded with soul, with will, with ideality. It contains an intoxicating vital sense, an intense thirst for the animal desire of life, but at the same time strict self-denial and reflexive self-discipline.* (Eklund 1970: 21)

That the art of painting and an interest in sport fit together well at this time is exemplified by another Finnish-Swede: Sigurd Frosterus, who in his collection of essays *Olikartade skönhetsvärden* takes up pure beauty and pure form. In this connection he touches on the game of tennis, which according to him is precisely characterised by being a "pure" game. He opposes the game to boxing and fencing, which have complicated rules for what one may and may not do, and in which it can be difficult to expose cheating and rule breaking, and to marathon races, shot-putting, and discus and javelin throwing, which are called "one-dimensional measurements of strength and suppleness". Tennis, on the other hand, with its clear form and its "transparency" is a beautiful sport, related to the pure work of art, and requires muscular as well as mental and emotional mastery

With its reference to physical as well as aesthetic beauty, this combination of formed wildness and a controlled thirst for life was attractive and fascinating to many of his contemporaries. The Stockholm Olympics reflected this new outlook on the body in many ways, while at the same time setting new ideas going as regards the view of the body and its democratic possibilities.

This new wave of enthusiasm was not just a fixed idea in the minds of philosophers, teachers and beaux-esprits. It also had a material basis. Up to the First World War the conception of time and space changed. Distances were conquered with the telegraph, telephone and radio, while at the same time space appears as a field of expansion for the ambitions of mankind (Kern 1994). It is dynamized. But this expansion beyond the encapsulated "Gemeinschaft" intimacy constantly threatens to run amok. The expansion therefore calls out to be curbed. The common denominator here becomes the spatial area, that is, the space which is so extended that it constitutes a field of development, but which at the same time is kept in check in the form of a demarcation. This can for instance be in the shape of a stadium, which is characterised by organic fullness with the possibility of filling the space with physical activity, and form, which indicates the framework for this activity and which within its boundaries allows the body to be brought into play to the utmost – yet in a controlled way.

After 1990 not only the educated and cultivated sons of the bourgeoisie frequented these new arenas, but also those of the working class (the girls were still long in coming). Visionary social democrats like A.C. Meyer in Denmark (who also wrote in *Vagten*) and the future Swedish Prime Minister Hjalmar Branting immediately realised the possibilities that sport gave the working class youth to show its strength. Here in the "pure" world of sport neither the social nor the political nor the economic environment played an important role. Only physical ability was decisive.

In the debate in the Swedish parliament on financial support for OL participants before the games in 1912, it also turns out that Branting has realised that sport contains possibilities for bringing the vigorous working class youth onto the same social map (Lindroth 1974). The strong, healthy, vital working class youth have in his view every possibility of demonstrating a new kind of "Swedishness" that is no longer characterised by toast speeches among the aristocracy and bourgeoisie, but rather of movement and physical activity: in healthy, vital sports folk with a working class background represent the new generation that is to conquer Sweden.

It is thus possible to kill two birds and more with one stone: one can confront the degeneration and thought of decadence, one can show that when the working class fights on equal terms it can easily take care of itself socially, and one can strike a blow for body and action as the common characteristic of mankind.

For this reason, the series of Swedish and Scandinavian victories at the Stockholm Olympics is presented as a sign of the new, youthful Scandinavia. English sports, the German cultivation of youth, and the young, vital and popular Scandinavia could go hand in hand here in a vision of the new international, democratic and popular Europe.

To be sure, this illusion collapsed two years later, but the vision of the popular, outdoorsy Scandinavia, which combined physical vitality with civilised and controlled corporality, survived – heralded among other things by the Stockholm Olympics. Here it was suspected that the body could achieve honour and respect as a field of development for the masses, offering people a world that had a value in itself with games, fun, and the pleasure of movement. Here they experienced that the body could be cultivated for its own sake without necessarily having to serve another cause. The body became, as Jonas Frykman has pointed out, a legitimate and pleasureful forum for forming experiences (Frykman 1993). Physical activities ranging from sport to athletics and from dance to jazz music to holiday and outdoor life became the way to acquire the possibilities of the new, modern welfare society, while at the same time this can also be said to have been created by virtue of these physical activities. One has experiences with one's body in an altogether non-martial way which was equally as far from military robot-like discipline, on the one hand, and wild and unmanageable recklessness on the other. Sport, dance and outdoor life helped create a peaceful nationalism in the name of modernity and welfare (Kayser Nielsen 1997a; 1997d). Gymnastics, athletics and exercise developed in the course of the 1930s to become the most quickly growing popular movement. It was part of the revolution of the body, "mightier than all political revolutions", as it says in a Swedish social-democratic periodical in 1934 (Frykman 1993: 172).

Perhaps it is this experience that caused the Scandinavian youth movement to develop in a different way than in Germany and England, where, as John B. Gillis has shown (Gillis 1974), the youth movement became strongly anti-modernistic and anti-urban. It is true that, thanks to strong German influence, it is possible also to trace signs of both anti-modernism and anti-urbanism within the youth movements in Finland and Denmark in the 1920s and '30s, but the democratic view of politics was after all victorious in these two countries, in that as far as Denmark was concerned the centrally positioned Grundtvigian movement, which was in the historically decisive middle field between right and left, unequivocally chose to form a political front against fascism, and inasmuch as the younger part of the movement was trying its best to ensure that modernity also enter the ranks of the Grundtvigians.

Solveig Bording conclusively expressed this new version of nationalism in 1929 in the magazine *Ungdom og Idræt* (Youth and athletics):

> *No one can survive on tradition without renewing it; our patriotism must also be renewed in us. And although it is not expressed in the same way as before, although we are perhaps more cautious in speaking about our Danish national feeling, about our love of our flag and our country, we can nevertheless fight for it, perhaps in a more everyday way.* (Ungdom og Idræt 1929, No. 12: 102)

Four years later, when Grundtvigian circles were animatedly discussing modern dance or folkdance, the following contribution on modern dance was made to the publication of the Danish Youth Associations, *Dansk Ungdom* (Danish youth):

> *Yet it follows the times and corresponds to them. The restlessness that is everywhere leaves its mark above all on the youth. When they need to relax at the end of a working day, it is no wonder that they prefer modern dance, with its smooth rhythm and music that has such a soothing effect on the nerves, rather than the old folk dances, which require the brain to work without pause in order to remember all the many steps and skips, so that after two hours of dancing one is more tired than after an entire day at work.* (Dansk Ungdom 1933: 79)

Subsequently, modern dance could gradually also be accepted in the Grundtvigian youth associations (Kayser Nielsen 1997e). The light temperament was victorious. But then, the sun had also shone so brightly in the light Swedish summer of 1912.

NORDIC TRACK AND FIELD IN THE INTERWAR YEARS: A COMPARISON

When the Swedish athletics trainer Carl Silfverstrand held a speech in 1930 at the Oslo Labour Party's festival for the city's youth, he was demonstrating an example of Nordic cooperation in the field of athletics. His very presence at the meeting was living proof that athletics in Scandinavia at this time was characterized by a sense of community and a shared history. Before this he had worked as a trainer and coach in both Denmark and Finland, and he had been a central figure in spreading athletics, partly by virtue of his work with training, partly because of his outspoken views about the difference between athletics and gymnastics.

It is this joint Nordic perspective that I shall consider here, although I shall emphasize the differences between the sporting traditions of the different countries rather than the similarities. The fact is that the Nordic countries in the inter-war period diverged radically as regards the perception and spread of athletics, and Denmark in particular differed from the other countries. This was an effect of the interaction between climate, social conditions, and sports policy. There is no question here of geographic determinism, but one cannot ignore the fact that the differing geographical conditions in the Nordic countries have had an influence on the history of sport in general and of athletics in particular, but this influence has always take place in interaction with factors of a social, political, and especially national kind.

A general outlook in the article is that the history of sport should always be viewed from a multifactorial perspective, with the relationship of athletics to nation-building and national identity playing a particularly important role. The thesis for which I shall argue is that nationalism has had a crucial impact on the shaping of the overall sports system in each of the Nordic countries, specifically in deciding which events would become popular in each country.

The opposition of gymnastics to athletics

From the very beginning, athletics – in the sense of track and field events – found itself in competition, chiefly with gymnastics. In all the Nordic countries from the turn of the century, people on the gymnastics side had expressed their scepticism about many sports, not least athletics.

In Sweden the conflict was between, on the one hand, men like Gustaf Nyblæus and Viktor Balck, and on the other hand the spokesmen of Ling gymnastics such as Mauritz Törngren from the Central Institute of Gymnastics (GCI) in Stockholm. Viktor Balck ("the father of Swedish sport") vehemently rejected the stiff and authoritarian gymnastics, especially the Swedish variant founded by Pehr Henrik Ling (Lindroth 1974: 197 ff.; Meinander 1994: 147 ff.), while the GCI, which trained teachers of physical education for the Swedish school system, criticized competitive sports for being based on incorrect physiological premises, irrational, and élitist – in short, morally and physically harmful (Lindroth 1993: 47).

Another anti-Lingian was headmaster of the Norra Real grammar school in Stockholm, Carl Svedelius, who was also a prominent athletics instructor. He emphasized the character-forming function of athletics (Meinander 1991), but he was just as discontented with the rigid didactic system of school gymnastics, based on neohumanist educational ideals, as Victor Balck was with Ling gymnastics. Svedelius's hobby horse was instead outdoor life, sports, and winter sports, for he saw here a potential to develop the modern, spontaneous individual who would simultaneously be a social being. In keeping with this, he was instrumental in reforming the school's gymnastics club into an athletics club, just as he had taken the initiative two years previously to arrange the school's annual winter trips to Jämtland, an institution that would later develop into the "sports holiday" that all Swedish schoolchildren have in February (Sörlin 1995). His overall goal was to develop individuals with a sense of communal responsibility in a modern society, and for this purpose he found athletics more useful than gymnastics. As we shall see below, his ideas did not become widespread until the inter-war years. At first society was not prepared for his ideas about athletics.

In Denmark the conflict between gymnastics and athletics was just as fierce, but here the advocates of gymnastics showed the greatest ardour. Here too, the gymnasts criticized the athletes for their one-sided cultivation of particular parts of the body, instead of applying oneself to the whole body. The reason was that essential feature of athletics that has haunted it ever since: specialization. In contrast, the aim of gymnastics was to shape the body in architectonic harmony, as an organic whole.

For contemporary gymnastics instructors this meant opposing English sport to continental European gymnastics. In a textbook on training from 1911, one of the spokesmen of Danish gymnastics, K.A. Knudsen, said:

> *The most important instrument today for the high physical education which some young people in England receive is still running; for that is the most significant thing in all ball games. … But however excellent running may be as an instrument for physical education, it is still not sufficient. Alongside the requirement of ensuring a vigorous metabolism, gymnastics has to fulfil another equally important requirement, namely, to shape the body into harmonious beauty, because only thus can one reach perfect beauty. Running cannot satisfy this demand; it is one-sided.* (Knudsen 1911: 37)

In other words, K.A. Knudsen's surprisingly modern view – that health is synonymous with physical beauty – leaves no room for running, which is perceived as something with a purely corporeal function. This difference between sports and gymnastics was perhaps never formulated as precisely as by the Finland-Swedish sports philosopher and publicist Artur Eklund. In his book *Idrottens filosofi* ("The Philosophy of Sport") from 1917 he points out that sport is concerned with expedience and utilitarianism, whereas the aim of gymnastics is beauty:

> *Gymnastics is consequently not directed outwards, does not seek a concrete result; instead it is directed inwards: movement, form become ends in themselves. From this follows the profound difference between the character of athletics and that of gymnastics. Whereas the former is extrovert, assaulting, ambitious, individualistic, gymnastics is composed, subdued, harmonious, bound by obedience to the demands of the teacher and the community.* (Eklund 1970 (1917): 27)

As we shall see below, this perception of gymnastics was also embraced by Carl Silfverstrand a few years later, but for him it was a reason to dissociate himself from gymnastics and to defend athletics.

Gymnastics and ball games in Denmark around 1900

The gymnasts had the same antipathy to ball games. Gymnastics showed an early tolerance of so-called "organized games", which also included ball games. At the same time, we may note an interesting phenomenon around the turn of the century, that a number of ball clubs in Denmark, especially in Jutland, were founded by people with their roots in the world of the folk high schools and hence people with a passion for what was called "Swedish" gymnastics. A suitable example is the village of Bøvling in north-west Jutland, one of the bastions of Grundtvigianism in Jutland. Here it was a teacher who took the initiative, having become interested in football during a period spent at Vestbirk High School (Alstrup 1950: 869). As a result, the local gymnastics club, founded in 1899, added ball games to the programme in 1901. There was no opposition here between folk high school, gymnastics, and football.

The same was true of Horne in western Jutland. Here it was Horne Football Club, as it was originally called (it was not until the late 1920s that the name was changed to the current Horne Sports Club), started in 1903 by Jørgen Rasmussen, who had taken a course for gymnastics instructors and had learned the game. The young people in the village could not satisfy their thirst for football in the gymnastics club, so they formed their own club with his assistance. So many people were interested that Horne in 1907 was able to field both a first team and a second team (Aggeboe and Vig Nielsen 1988: 12 f.).

In the Vejen-Askov area in south Jutland, where Denmark's most famous folk high school with a tradition of training gymnastics instructors is located, there was likewise a close link between football and the folk high school, with people from the same circle being active in both spheres. The Danish folk high schools were rarely negative to new ideas, and since sport has been a way to attract young people in large numbers, they were not unsympathetic to football. As regards Vejen, we know that the people associated with the folk high school in Askov helped to introduce football there (Kayser Nielsen 1994c).

In this connection, it is interesting to dwell on the fact that two of the three core areas from which football spread over Jutland around 1900 – the district around Vejen-Brørup-Holsted and the area between Varde and Tarm – were also known for their active training of gymnastics instructors. "Football villages" such as Vejen, Brørup, Outrup, Fåborg, Tistrup, Horne, and Holsted were also among the villages and station towns that most frequently had gymnasts on courses for platoon commanders (Bruhn 1979).

Sport and nation-building

When antipathy to athletics was very strong in Scandinavia at the end of the nineteenth century, it was probably due to the distinctive Nordic tradition of physical enlightenment – with roots going back to the continental European philanthropic body culture – which had been fervent throughout the nineteenth century. This physically oriented popular enlightenment was closely associated with the nationalism that in Scandinavia, as elsewhere in Europe, used the charismatic leaders of physical culture as an element in nation-building. In Germany, "Turnvater" Jahn played an important role in this regard (Eisenberg 1996). In Denmark the dominant figures were first Nachtegall, with his close ties to the royal family (Kayser Nielsen 1996), and then Grundtvig. Sweden had Pehr Henrik Ling, and later his son Hjalmar Ling.

In all these cases there were people who used gymnastics (and to some extent swimming) as an instrument to build up a martial and national frame of mind. Whereas the Anglo-Saxon world up to the First World War could use athletics, sports involving physical strength, and ball games for nationalist propaganda (Veitch 1985), on the Continent, and hence also in Scandinavia, it was primarily gymnastics that was intimately associated with nationalism. Sports were considered non-Nordic and international.

As a result, this set a different agenda for athletics, which could thus be criticized for its bodily specialization and for its non-nationalism. In other words, sport, and hence athletics, could not be used in Scandinavia as an instrument for nation-building, since the role was already filled. Yet this is not the whole truth. For we must bear in mind that Nordic nation-building was pursued according to different models. Until the end of the Napoleonic Wars, Scandinavia consisted of two kingdoms: Sweden-Finland and Denmark-Norway. These two unions – the effects of which still make themselves felt – were broken up in 1809, when Sweden had to give up Finland, which became a Grand Duchy of the Russian Empire, and acquired Norway as compensation. It was not until 1905 that Norway became an independent nation, while Finland had to wait until 1917 and the dissolution of tsarist Russia.

This situation created very different conditions for nation-building in the Nordic countries. Well into the twentieth century in Sweden and Denmark, gymnastics was able to maintain its position as the physical culture most closely associated with nationalism, whereas the Norwegians could not allow the Swedes with their gymnastics to take out a patent on the corporeal representation of Norwegianness. The Norwegians therefore had to go their own way. They found the solution in skiing. Nineteenth-century physical nationalism was thus expressed to a large extent in skiing, as recent research into the history of skiing in Norway has shown (Christensen 1993), and in 1934 the Norwegian gymnastics instructor Ottar Ystad, who worked in Denmark, was able to declare that "Although football and athletics are widespread in Norway, they are nevertheless surpassed by skiing" (Ystad 1934: 35).

The special case of Finland

In Finland the situation was partly different. Here too the people had to fight for national independence throughout the nineteenth century, but whereas the Norwegians for national reasons could hardly adopt the Ling gymnastics from Sweden, the situation was different in Finland, since Ling gymnastics represented what had been lost when Finland was swallowed up by Russia. However, this picture was confused by one specific factor, namely, that the struggle for national independence in Finland was linked to the struggle for the Finnish language. The Finns put it like this: "We cannot be Swedes, we do not want to be Russians – let us therefore be Finns."

To put it another way, from about 1860 Finnish national senti-
ment became Fennomania, in that it was also opposed to the Swedish-speaking upper class. Like Danish Grundtvigianism, it lacked
a formal organization and rather had the character of an élitist
movement which derived its legitimacy by professing to act on
behalf of the people (Stenius 1992). A number of Swedish-speaking
families, in solidarity with the aspirations of the young Fennoma-
niacs, changed their names from Swedish to Finnish (for example,
from Forsman to Koskinen, from Gallén to Gallén-Kallela), and the
composer Sibelius, who came from a family of Swedish-speaking offi-
cials, endeavoured to create a national Finnish musical iconography.
Finnish was regarded as the heart of the nation, whereas Swedish
was perceived as its stiffening shell (Högnäs 1995: 28). This Fennomania made it difficult to automatically adopt the Swedish Ling
gymnastics as a national representation. As in Norway, they had
to go their own way, and it was competitive sport that triumphed
(Laine 1992).

Here we should bear in mind, however, that the nation-building of the independent Finland in the twentieth century has had
a very different character from Norwegian nation-building. First,
it began later than in Norway, at a time when sport had made its
breakthrough, at least in the cities. Second, it was of a much more
dramatic character, in that Finland was the only Nordic country to
be torn by a civil war. Third, all through the inter-war years there
was the real or imagined threat of the communist and collectivist
Soviet Union to the east. This created a rather different agenda for
the demands for a national bodily representation in the twentieth
century than in the other Nordic countries.

At the same time, one must bear in mind the geographical conditions. It could easily have happened that the Finns, like the Norwegians, chose skiing as their national symbol, but the period in which
the new independent nation had to build an identity now had other
options in the form of modern sport. At the same time, ideological
considerations could have influenced the choice between individual
sports and team sports. The fact that the Soviet "*kolkhoz* mentality"
was regarded as one of the main enemies was not without significance; it was partly for political reasons that individual sports were
valued more highly in the politically inflammable interwar period,

like the athletics training we see depicted in a novel by Väinö Linna about the right-wing-oriented Civil Guards. It might be appropriate here to quote the editor of the newsletter of the Danish Gymnastics Association (DDG), A. Pedersen Dømmestrup, whose statement in 1930 testifies to the affinity between the Grundtvigian gymnastics tradition in Denmark and the physical culture of the Fennomaniac heritage:

> *The young people of Finland engage in athletics as the youth of Den-*
> *mark indulge in gymnastics. Young Finns, especially in the country-*
> *side, practise athletics in the evenings and in their spare time, not in a*
> *stadium, since the distances are too great, but outside the farm, where*
> *they have their daily work.* (Pedersen Dømmestrup 1930: 291)

Other aspects of human geography are seen here, including the fact that there was still very little urbanization in Finland in the inter-war period. The urban population concentration in the towns was small, and even in the countryside the form of settlement in most of Finland comprised isolated farms rather than true villages of the kind found in Denmark and southern Sweden. If one wanted to compete with others, one had to travel – sometimes long distances. This once again favoured individual sports in which one could com-pete against oneself.

If we consider the late date of independent nation-building in Finland, at a time when sport was catching on, the factors all point in the direction of athletics, in other words, the great individual sport of the twentieth century, and it is characteristic that Finland's most splendid international sporting triumphs have been in athlet-ics, especially in events that are suited to personal training, such as long-distance running and the javelin. If we look at world athletics in 1934, for example, we see that the records for races from 5 km upwards and for the discus (for both hands) and the javelin were held by Finns. Measured in terms of world records, Finland that year was the second-best athletics nation in the world, after the USA.

Collectivist Danish sports

The fact that athletics has found it much more difficult to catch on in Norway as the preferred individual sport can be explained to some extent by the close link between sport and nationalism which favoured skiing, as we saw above, but also by geographical conditions: both the human geography, as Norway is also a country of isolated farms and relatively little urbanization, and the physical geography, with the long winters inviting people to go skiing and skating.

It is trickier to understand why athletics has always found it difficult to gain a firm foothold in Denmark. Even back in 1909 the first composite work on Danish sport declares that Danish athletes appear to form the rear guard in the "international athletic army" (Grønfeldt 1909: 27). Otherwise the climatic conditions should be good enough, with the mild weather and short winters, so that there is practically no competition from winter sports. But climate alone is not decisive. Other factors are involved.

We must bear in mind that athletics from the very beginning found it hard to secure a position as a consequence of the opposition of gymnastics. This opposition did not affect football as much, and this also impeded the spread of athletics, since ball games as a summer sport could also benefit from the favour of the gymnastics side.

Athletics did nevertheless catch on gradually. It is perhaps due to the nature of athletics: the combination of strength and speed, and the obvious potential for sportification in the direction of competition, with the emphasis on performance, records, and standardized tables, was well suited to the pulse of the cities, with their ordered yet bustling life. A statement in the 1922 annual of the Danish Athletics Association (DIF), again by Carl Silfverstrand, is significant:

> *Whatever one undertakes in life ... one must start at the bottom – in other words, there must be a system in it.* (Dansk Idræts Forbund 1923)

It was not by chance that Silfverstrand came to Denmark. The fact of the matter was that athletics badly needed coaches, since this discipline requires more technical skill than many other branches of sport, and since the practitioner is often left to himself or just a few other athletes. It was therefore decided in 1918 that assistance should be sought in Sweden, which was much further advanced on the coaching side as well. As a result, William Kriegsmann was hired as a trainer in the Copenhagen area, while Olle Svedlund moved to Jutland. There was no great success, however, but in 1922 the DIF decided to look for help in Sweden once again. The well-known athletics coach Carl Silfverstrand was therefore employed full-time (Faxøe 1934: 201). He was an international authority who had worked as a trainer in Helsinki in 1919-20, and he would later play a major role in Finnish athletics with his successful work for the ambitious Kiffen club in Helsinki (Björkman 1997: 56 and 87). In Denmark, however, he did not enjoy the same success.

In the midst of the First World War, in 1917, ten new clubs joined the DIF, making a total of 62 clubs with about 8,000 members. The future thus looked promising, but if we look at the number of members of the association in 1945, we see that the number had not risen to more than about 13,500 active members, in 209 clubs. In other words, there was a tendency to decentralization, with many small clubs each with a relatively small number of members (Kayser Nielsen 1995c). This could hardly benefit the growth of élite athletics.

This development towards the decentralization of sports, and hence the spread over the whole country of sport as a popular pursuit, was one of the characteristics of inter-war sport in Denmark, and thus of athletics. Another characteristic was the increased professionalization. On pictures of athletics from before the First World War one can see that technique and style were indifferent. Hurdle races, for instance, were run in a style that seems haphazard and inappropriate. This was changed between the wars. To put it in positive terms, athletic style was made homogeneous and efficient, thus improving performance. To put it in negative terms, the diversity was eliminated and strict uniformity was introduced as sportification proceeded, with its emphasis on standardization, planning, and performance.

A third characteristic feature of athletics in the interwar years was the hero worship that especially accompanied the achievements of the best runners. The population, not least in the provincial towns, worshipped their local heroes with a mixture of enthusiasm, pride, and awe. They were seen as representatives of what a town could produce, and as representatives of the rapid development in both living standard and technical skills, so that they also became symbols of progress, growth, and development. Here athletics contributed more than any other branch of sport, with its combined display of one individual's biological capacity, will-power, and diligent training.

Despite all this, athletics never became the same mass sport in Denmark as it was in the other Nordic countries, especially Finland. The 13,500 active athletes pale in comparison to the number of handball players: in 1938 there were already about 28,000 active handball players, twice the number of athletes, and by 1948 there were 75,000 handball players organized in clubs (Kayser Nielsen 1997b).

As early as 1921, the Old Boys club held the first handball tournament in the Sports Hall in Copenhagen, and when this event was taken over by the Copenhagen Handball Association in 1931, the foundation was laid for a nationwide tournament, although because of the war this was not actually held until 1947.

Many of these handball players had started in athletics. The fact is that, when handball was "discovered" in earnest in the 1920s, it was one of the divisions of the athletics association. This was the case, for example, in Jutland, where people doing athletics in the Aarhus Fremad club became the first Jutland handball champions. They had discovered that handball (in its indoor version) was an effective way to stay in shape during the winter months when athletics lay dormant. This was a dangerous discovery: 1935 saw the foundation of the Danish Handball Association when it broke away from the athletics association. This was the start of the gradual decline of athletics in the towns.

The situation in the countryside was different. Here DIF, the principal organization engaged in sport, was not very strong. Sports here were dominated from 1930 onwards by the two broadly based organizations DDSG&I and DDG, the first of which was started as rifle and gymnastics movement which later included sports on its programme, while the latter concentrated on gymnastics. In other words, clubs in both organizations emphasized indoor winter activities. Little attention was devoted to summer activities. However, both these organizations encountered serious crises in the first half of the 1930s, partly because of the general depression, partly because the narrow range of activities was ultimately too boring for young people. The problem was not solved until the organizations began to encourage summer sports as well, and here it was handball that became important, while athletics hardly figured at all. Handball was introduced in many places by gymnastics instructors and trainers who, on completing their courses at the folk high schools, returned to their villages with new ideas, including handball.

We can return again to geographical conditions: in densely populated Denmark, with short distances between villages, it was easy to get up a team in every village and easy for them to cycle to the neighbouring village to play against another team. This situation did not make it any easier for athletics to catch on. And for those who wanted to engage in an individual sport, badminton appeared in the 1930s as one possibility. This sport, which required little in terms of material or space, and which could also be played in schools, hotels, and especially in the parish halls that Denmark is so famous for, enjoyed such a strong breakthrough that it is without doubt one of the striking successes in Danish sports history. This crushed the last chance for athletics to gain a real foothold in Denmark. It is scarcely by chance that, apart from Niels Holst-Sørensen in the 1940s and Gunnar Nielsen in the 1950s (and he was trained for several years by the Finn (!) Ingmar Björkman), Denmark has never bred any world-class athletes. The potential talent was simply too small, since the base was so narrow.

Sweden – in the middle

In the years 1917-27 an annual three-way athletics event was contested between Sweden, Norway, and Denmark. Denmark always finished last, with the result that they gave up in 1927 and instead competed against the Swedish province of Skåne, leaving Sweden and Norway to fight for first place – and Sweden usually won. But why was Sweden stronger than its Nordic neighbours? We can find one possible answer in the xenophobic description of the Olympic Games in Stockholm in 1912, at which the Swedes won great triumphs; it was written by the author Carl G. Laurin a few years later:

> *Sweden was victorious because our people since ancient times have been healthy, tall, not too rich and not too poor. Swedes have only rarely suffered from the pauperism that gnaws at city workers in England and France. Swedes do not develop rheumatism as a result of freezing with cold, as people do in other countries. Herring and potatoes, firewood and fresh air, at least outdoors, have been available for centuries.* (Laurin 1917: 175 f.)

This biological and environmental explanation was typical of the times, but we may suspect that the quotation above from Silfverstrand, about the value of systematic training, is closer to the truth. However, this does not change the fact that the Olympic Games in Stockholm in 1912 were the starting signal for the breakthrough of modern sports in Sweden. They were as important for the democratization of sport in Sweden as the Stockholm Exhibition of 1930 was for the democratization of leisure. There is thus reason to suppose that the decidedly favourable attitude of the Swedish government to sport in the years before the First World War was reinforced by the Olympic Games. In any case, the first state grants to sport were allocated in 1913 (Lindroth 1974: 279 ff.), just as the army was involved: the first instructions in training for the participant took place in the Swedish Artillery Regiment's Riding House autumn 1910 (Persson and Pettersson 1995: 70).

In these years Sweden was industrialized and urbanized in earnest, which helped to further the breakthrough of sport as a popular movement. In 1919 the Swedish Sports Confederation (RF) had 93,000 members. In the 1920s the figure rose to about 200,000 members engaged in organized sports. In the course of the 1930s another 200,000 were added, so that RF in 1940 could count almost 400,000 members. This figure was doubled once again in the 1940s (Lindroth 1987).

Of these practitioners of sport, athletes made up the largest group up to the 1920s, when a certain stagnation set in. In 1920 almost a third (29 per cent) of clubs affiliated to RF pursued athletics, with an even geographical distribution over the country, whereas football accounted for 20 per cent of the clubs and skiing 18 per cent (Lindroth 1987: 52 ff.). Here we have of course one significant explanation why Swedish athletics enjoyed its first period of glory in the years leading up to 1920 (the second period came in the 1940s).

Other factors were at work, however: in the 1890s athletics was already the branch of sport that was developing most vigorously in terms of the number of practitioners, the amount of public attention, and the fixation on results and records. Sports newspapers such as *Tidning för Idrott* and *Start* both gave extravagant publicity to athletic records (Cederquist 1996: 28). This also strengthened Swedish athletics. Being firmly organized in the rational and democratic RF also benefited athletics. It was likewise important for athletics in Sweden that the new Swedish industrial bourgeoisie was favourably disposed to the new sports movement in general and to athletics in particular: in 1916 the top men in Swedish business and industry donated a very large sum of money to instruction in athletics. Both sectors of society could thus assemble in their orientation to results and competition.

At the same time, Swedish nationalism changed character. As Sweden became social democratic, the old militaristic patriotism of the nineteenth century was succeeded by a modern "welfare nationalism", based not so much on the obedient as on the collaborating individual. Correspondingly, young people now no longer perceived themselves as the ideological storm troops of nationalism but simply as young people. The puritanical bent was replaced by modern mass culture. The large youth movements became focal points for social activities – places where young people could meet and have fun (Berggren 1997: 251 f.).

This was to favour sports (athletics and ball games) at the expense of Ling gymnastics, which now ceased to be a popular sport. The traditional gymnastics instructor and his world, in which "the ideals are as upright as the figures: flags flap, the line are straight, and the upper lips are stiff" (Sörlin 1995: 92), disappeared, to be replaced by the at once playing and competing sporty, outdoor person, who tested the new social-liberal society in and with his body (Frykman 1992; Frykman 1993). Once again we can turn to Silfverstrand, who claimed in the 1922 annual of the DIF that, whereas the sporting individual can move "free and unforced", it is different with the gymnast:

He stands under the influence of a different will, that of the person directing the team. This means that his movements do not have the same freedom, they become more forced, in particular during a display. (Dansk Idræts-Forbund 1923: 68)

He added that

A gymnast who engages in athletics during the summer can to a certain extent free himself from this "stiffness". (Dansk Idræts-Forbund 1923: 69)

With these words, Silfverstrand interpreted the view that was to become part of the collective mentality of sport in the interwar years. Sport was more in keeping with the social-liberal societal ideal than authoritarian gymnastics.

In organizational terms too, Sweden differed from Denmark, which, besides DIF, the body responsible for sport, had two other organizations which together were almost as big as DIF, and which took charge of gymnastics. In Sweden they had RF as the only significant organization for sport.

The pronounced public interest in sport and outdoor life in Sweden in the inter-war period also favoured the construction of sports facilities. The most up-to-date technological advances could be utilized in the form of cinder tracks, in which sand and gravel were mixed with granulated carbon or brick. This gave a much harder surface, thus ensuring a better foothold. The Swedish cinder tracks in the 1940s and 1950s had the reputation of being the best in the world, in other words, the fastest (Moen 1992: 15 f.). It was not least these technical factors that allowed the Swedes Gunder Hägg and Arne Andersson to set one world record after the other in the war years; in addition, of course, there was less competition during these years from the war-torn world outside neutral Sweden.

In Sweden, as in Finland, there was at the same time a systematic drive to develop talent and training, which was further encouraged by the early – by European standards – construction of large indoor athletics arenas with internationally recognized dimensions. Against this background, it is hardly surprising that Swedish athletics, right up to our own days and the high jumper Patrik Sjöberg, has been able to assert itself in the world élite.

Conclusion

In a comparative view on Nordic sports history this chapter raises the question as to why athletics in the interwar period provided an adequate national representation of Finland and, partly, Sweden, but not of Denmark and Norway. The answer to the question is found in a combination of the geographical, political and socio-historical circumstances which, in spite of several resemblances, also differed strikingly in the Nordic countries.

Sweden has never reached the same level as Finland, but Swedish athletics has always been much stronger than athletics in Denmark, and a good deal stronger than athletics in Norway. The annual athletic contest between Sweden and Finland (*Finnkampen*) has always attracted huge numbers of spectators and the outcome has never been a foregone conclusion. In the 1930s competition between the two countries was so tough (this was in the middle of Paavo Nurmi's heyday) that sometimes the contest had to be cancelled because the spectators were too chauvinistic. On the other hand, during the Second World War the public walking competitions between the two countries also made it clear that the Finns were masters.

As part of the campaign to build up military preparedness in both countries, Sweden was to compete in spring 1941 with Finland in a "people's international" walking race. The aim was to see which country could muster the most citizens to walk ten kilometres. As a consequence of the demographic difference between the two countries – the population of Finland was only half that of Sweden – it was agreed that the number of Finnish participants would be multiplied by two. There was no need for this mathematical stratagem, however: about a million Swedes came out to walk, but a million and a half Finns walked the ten kilometres. Once again it was shown that Finland was the leading Nordic country in athletics, at both élite and popular levels. The situation has not changed today. Nor has Denmark's position at the bottom of the Nordic league changed: we have to import runners from Africa if we want Olympic medals.

HANDBALL IN RURAL DENMARK IN THE 1930s

In many ways the years between the two World Wars saw the ultimate breakthrough of sport in Denmark. Gymnastics had been introduced during the period before the First World War – in the countryside by way of the folk high schools, and in the towns via the gymnastic institutes. This period also witnessed the breakthrough of the English-influenced competitive sport, which was still an exclusively urban phenomenon in the era of the Modern Breakthrough. So what was still missing at the time of the First World War was the spread of sport in rural districts. This finally came in the 1920s and 1930s, mainly because many of the gymnastic clubs began to stagnate around 1930. Other sports, especially handball and football and the rapidly spreading badminton, came like a breath of fresh air, saving numerous gymnastic and athletic clubs from collapse.

There were several reasons for the stagnation of the gymnastic clubs around 1930. There is a great deal to suggest that their decline was part of a general crisis among clubs and associations at this time, which not only afflicted rural gymnastic clubs but also associations as a whole all over Denmark. Furthermore, there was the general economic crisis which meant that many people could not afford to take part in club life, and in this regard we must also bear in mind a concrete problem that the Depression had for the rural people, i.e. young hired men and women needed to change jobs more often. This of course weakened the continuity of club life, especially if we remember that many of these farm- hands and maids were board members in the athletic clubs. When they had to move after just six months, whether to help out at home or to find better employment elsewhere, or even to move to a town in the hope of finding their fortune there, the clubs had to look for new board members. This might not have been a serious problem when servants changed their place of employment on the 1st May (as was the common practice at the time in Denmark), since no one was doing gymnastics at that time of the year anyway, but if people moved on the 1st November (the other "official" date for changing job) when club activities were supposed to be in full swing again for the winter season, then the clubs could have had difficulties.

Finally, we cannot ignore the fact that many young people, not just in the towns, were simply beginning to find gymnastics too boring. In many places Niels Bukh's jumping gymnastics had not caught on, and the stiff and static "Swedish" gymnastics found it difficult to attract enough people. Besides, gymnastics was restricted to the wintertime, which meant that there were no summer activities, and perhaps the clubs generally had too many admonishing tutors and pig-headed drill instructors (Kayser Nielsen 1995a; 1995c).

The breakthrough of sport

The foregoing may also explain the breakthrough of other types of sport in the countryside in place of gymnastics. Sport was more dynamic and more in keeping with the urban culture that was beginning to attract many young rural people in the interwar years: they also had radios in their living rooms, buses and cinemas. The peasantry had been modernized in a distinctively Danish way during the previous generation, thanks partly to the village halls and mission houses. Therefore, although we are justified in speaking of a special Danish agrarian modernity, this was now replaced by state initiatives in the direction of a shared national culture (in the form of radio) and by private capitalist entertainment initiatives such as cinemas and weekly magazines. And sport fitted into this picture perfectly, with its speed and flair, it competition and performance.

Another important factor was that sport was able to bring the two genders together in the summer half of the year. In the heyday of gymnastics the rule had generally been for young people to wait for each other outside the village hall in the snow and slush until the gymnastics was finished so that a lad could walk his girl home. With the coming of sport, the picture changed. The long summer evenings could now be used to the full, and there were activities for both boys and girls, which meant that they could watch each other. As a rule, and for practical reasons, handball practice for girls and football practice for boys was held on the same evening, and some boys played handball too, which meant that boys and girls had a shared interest. This was very different from peeping through a keyhole in the village hall when the girls were doing gymnastics (Gjøde Nielsen 1994: 112). A light now shone over the country!

In addition a new phenomenon presented itself, the "sporting festival", which was held on Sundays when people had a free day. Teams competed with each other to win badges which could be pinned on their club flag. Whether a team played at home or went to a neighbouring village to play, it meant a broadening of experience in relation to the closed world of gymnastics. Not only were there the actual sporting activities, which could give rise to all kinds of comparison, but there were also the dances to the music of a live band in the village hall that followed the matches. The "sweetheart market" was thus considerably expanded and boys and girls could mix more easily. In a picture from the Gårslev Sports Club one can see a pair of shorts in the foreground, while a frock is hanging out to air in the background. The picture was taken at a sports event one summer in Kollemorten, at the end of the 1940s judging by the clothes. The young people from Gårslev were more than 50 km from home here. In the interwar years people were content with shorter distances, but the situation was the same. The erotic dimension in the 1930s is a significant part of the breakthrough of sport between the wars. And it was significant that the girls began to play handball. Now the two sexes could size each other up while practising and playing matches.

Rural girls get going

The breakthrough of handball in the countryside in the 1930s encountered obstacles however. Initially, many club leaders were highly sceptical about sport and competition. Even among those who practised sport there was some hesitation, particularly among the boys. In many places it was the girls who took the initiative, while the boys viewed handball as "a girl's game", and one to which they would not "stoop" as long as they had their football! The interest in handball was so great among girls that there are examples of servant girls negotiating terms of employment and making it a condition that they should be free in the evenings to play handball (Lyngaa 1995: 5). At Horne in West Jutland the first real handball leader was a young girl who had been to Ollerup Gymnastics College and learnt the rules and training methods (Lyngaa 1995: 5). When the Melby-Liseleje Sports Club in North Zealand was founded in 1936, the statutes declared that "The sports for male members are football and gymnastics, and for female members handball and gymnastics". At Klokkerholm in Vendsyssel, girls played handball from 1934, while boys did not start until 1945. We find the same pattern in a place like Hoven in West Jutland: in the late 1920s girls began to play eleven-a-side handball on big pitches, partly following the rules of football, after which the seven-a-side game caught on in the mid-1930s; the men did not start until 1946. Elsewhere, however, men did not have the same scruples.

At Drantum, south of Herning, gymnastics and handball were pursued together from the start under the auspices of the Gymnastics Club, with gymnastics displays, sports festivals, and handball matches being central concerns of the club during the season. At Søvind, between Horsens and Odder, the game gained a foothold at the start of the 1930s, and by 1936 they had a paid coach, who received 65 kroner for a whole summer season. Likewise, at Trelde near Fredericia, the game caught on in 1936, with a calf-enclosure behind the school as the pitch. It was introduced by a farmer's son who had spent a year and a half at Ollerup and learnt the game there. At the same time, this shows that the thesis so often argued in Danish sports history – the opposition of gymnastics and sport – is not entirely true as regards sport in practice. Perhaps scholars have been dazzled by the contrast between the elegant gymnasts and the beer-drinking footballers and ignored the fact that other sports were played too. Quite apart from the fact that many clubs, such as the example from Melby-Liseleje above, had both football and gymnastics on the programme for the same members, handball often served as a bridge between the two wings.

This was true in particular after the two major national athletics organizations, De Danske Gymnastikforeninger (DDG, The Danish Gymnastics Clubs) and De Danske Skytte-, Gymnastik- og Idrætsforeninger (DDSG&I, The Danish Shooting, Gymnastics and Athletics Clubs), adopted handball as one of their sporting activities in the 1930s. Here too, as we shall see, there was some hesitation, but there was also a great interest in new activities which could breathe new life into the clubs.

Let us therefore see what happened, concentrating on the situation in DDG.

The beginnings in 1929

We can start in 1929. In that year Charles Hansen from Bornholm wrote in a spring issue of the magazine *Ungdom og Idræt* (Young People and Athletics): "If we want to come into contact with young people, we have to look for them where it is easiest to find them" (*Ungdom og Idræt* 1929/17: 161). The problem was that there was too little on offer in the summertime to satisfy the sporting interests of young people. When spring was in the air, the gymnastics season came to an end, so what was left? For many young men the problem was solved by turning to football. In the summer, therefore, we find many of the young people in the world of football. Charles Hansen considered this unfortunate, however, because of the tone prevailing there; it was not always of a kind that had an "improving" effect on young people and this had led many gymnasts to believe that gymnastics and ball games were incompatible. This did not need to be the case, Charles Hansen wrote: "well-led ball games are just as estimable as gymnastics." However, football did not appear to have much of a chance, as there was scarcely any possibility of "improvement" in that sport. Luckily, however, football was not the only ball game. There was also basketball, hockey – and handball.

This was how the ball started rolling. The debate about handball as a part of "national" sports could begin. It was to last about ten years, but it ended in an almost unconditional victory for handball. At first, however, there was no great response, so in the first issue of the magazine in 1930, by which time Charles Hansen had come to Stevns Folk High School, he tried again, pointing out that he was by no means seeking to disregard gymnasttics (*Ungdom og Idræt* 1930/1: 5). He argued that both gymnastics and ball games should be seen as instruments in the service of education, but he was not blind to the widespread scepticism about ball games, because of the violence in these sports. Nevertheless, in the right circumstances ball games could ensure their practitioners "both better mastery of their limbs and better mastery of their whole content of moods, thoughts, words, and deeds."

Civilizing the rules

These clarifications appear to have done the trick, for the following year, in summer 1931, the co-editor of *Ungdom og Idræt*, A. Pedersen Dømmestrup, began to take a serious interest in the matter. He too was aware that football did not enjoy the support of the leaders of DDG, but he pointed out that there were other ball games, which into the bargain were "more agreeable" and "much easier to make work well" (*Ungdom og Idræt* 1931/23: 206), after which he described the rules of handball in detail. This was a remarkable step, since Dømmestrup was not just anybody. Besides being one of the editors of the magazine, he was employed at Ollerup and was one of the more farsighted and influential ideologists. When he backed Charles Hansen's idea by outlining the rules of the game (in the eleven-a-side version), his article had considerable weight, partly because of his position, partly because he thus helped to end ignorance about the game. In comparison with Holger Nielsen's and R.H. Ernst's time, a few revisions had made the game much more "civilized". The rough rugby-like elements were eliminated, and the rules allowed the game to be played in a more technical and tactical manner. Readers of the magazine could now observe this for themselves, and they could see that the game differed radically from football, in that there was not so much emphasis on muscle power.

All in all, football was often a stumbling block in the national clubs. It may have been the special tone of football that led both DDG and DDSG&I to take good time to think the matter over, before deciding to adopt handball. One of the issues discussed at the DDSG&I annual general meeting at Ollerup in 1932 was how to raise the ethical level of football, for example, by introducing a rule that swearing should result in a free kick for the other side (Jensen 1981: 27).

It was therefore of great significance that Dømmestrup so un-equivocally supported handball, and his support brought results. In the spring of 1933, *Ungdom og Idræt*, No. 18, declared that: "Handball has gradually acquired more and more practitioners in the districts" (*Ungdom og Idræt* 1933/18: 211) and that DDG in the meantime had set up a three-man committee – including Dømmestrup as a member – with the aim of compiling a uniform set of rules, based on the rules of DIF and the Skåne Gymnastics Association.

There was a softening of attitudes in DIF, but not in DDSG&I, which is perhaps evident from the fact that the next issue of the magazine published an article about English sport by the well-known sports teacher and leader, the headmaster Maigaard from Nakskov (*Ungdom og Idræt* 1933/19: 221 f.). This is a remarkable article in that Maigaard points out that English sport derives from the popular games and sports of Europe, and that the specifically English feature consists of adapting the forms and rules to suit the modern age. It was thus not a fundamental threat to the sport of the people, if only the leadership assumed responsibility for the correct development and elaboration of the sports.

At the national meeting of DDSG&I at Ollerup in 1935, the consequences of this were drawn. Sport was included for the first time, represented by events such as swimming, handball, basketball, and football. Handball received the greatest support, with forty matches to be played in both men's and women's classes. With this, handball had really come in from the cold (Jensen 1981: 31). It also meant a new sporting ambition. In the DDSG&I magazine, *Dansk Idræt*, for 1934, No. 13, the chairman of Sorø County urged the branches to send players to the joint training in Slagelse, so that Sorø could acquit itself well at the national meeting at Ollerup (*Dansk Idræt* 1934/13).

Between character development and coaching

The question of the right leadership was in focus in the ensuing years until the Second World War. It is interesting that in 1935 there were two important articles in *Ungdom og Idræt*, one about "Sport and Character Development", the other about "Coaching in Handball". In the first of these, Thøgersen points out that it is not enough that a sport should be "wholesome for the body"; it must also, as Charles Hansen had declared back in 1930, be wholesome for the character: it was essential to train will-power and the ability to cooperate, that is, "to submit to the common task" (*Ungdom og Idræt* 1935/12: 143).

From the other article we learn that DDG in May 1935 took the initiative for a meeting at Holbæk on coaching in handball, for "drill instructors and other interested parties". The meeting

was led by Poul Jørgensen, lecturer at the National Gymnastic Institute, who was the prime authority in the field. In 1933 he had
published the first edition of his *Vejledning i Haandbold* (Guide to
Handball), and was now working on the second edition (which did
not appear until 1938). This article is by another important figure in
DDG, K. Kristensen Killemose from Vallekilde Folk-High School;
he and Dømmestrup were to be the two most influential advocates
of handball in the DDG ranks in the 1930s. But the article is also
remarkable for the way that handball is now obviously regarded as
a sport requiring coaches rather than leaders. In other words, the
emphasis is more on the purely physical side, with a concentration
on techniques and tactics, rather than the character-forming importance of the game.

The debate continued in the winter of 1936, but now there was
a further incentive for DDG to adopt handball, namely, that the
so-called ball clubs were already busy playing it, and "we already
know only too well the motto of these clubs: it is fight, fight, fight",
as L.B. Hansen from Kirkeby puts it (*Ungdom og Idræt* 1936/3: 31).
There is some acceptance of competition, but still with an emphasis
on character formation: sport should never develop into sport solely
for the sake of sport. We have to save young people from the sporting danger, we must swallow the bitter pill and include handball in
the programme but at the same time make sure that it is not played
for its own sake as a purely physical activity.

This issue became increasingly central for DDG in the course
of the 1930s. (Skjerk 2001: 326 ff.). In the chairman's report to the
annual general meeting at Esbjerg in 1936 we read of the growing
shortage of drill instructors, and that gymnastics was developing into
"gymnastics and nothing else" (*Ungdom og Idræt* 1936/11: 126). While
its great intrinsic value was acknowledged, it was felt that it should
not be allowed to stand alone. Killemose of Vallekilde reports that
the élite gymnasts only come to the gymnastics a couple of evenings
before a display; this implies that they cannot be bothered to take
part in the laborious training of the ordinary gymnasts. And with
this already being a problem for gymnastics, what could be expected
in such a new sport as handball? Would it not mean heightened
difficulty in ensuring that it was kept free from a tendency to pure
corporeality? These thoughts appear to have concerned many gym-

nasts during these years. Many speakers at the meeting wondered whether it was defensible at all to embark on something new, when there was a risk that gymnastics could develop into a purely élite activity.

Towards common rules

Dømmestrup did not have this kind of scruples. He presented his report on the work of the handball committee (*Ungdom og Idræt* 1936/11: 130), in which he was able to announce that DDSG&I had been approached in the autumn of 1935 with a view to cooperation on the rules of handball, but without success. As we see from *Dansk Idræt*, DDSG&I used the rules that applied at Ollerup Gymnastics College (*Dansk Idræt* 1935/7). On the other hand, the approach to the Danish Handball Association was warmly welcomed, after which DDSG&I also wanted to join in. As a result, in the spring of 1936 there was a movement away from the situation in which DIF, DDG, DDSG&I, and Ollerup each had its own set of rules. In other words, handball was becoming a shared national sport, as we see from an announcement in *Ungdom og Idræt* in summer 1937, to the effect that a match had been played for the "National Fyn Championship" between Svendborg from DDSG&I and Tarup from DDG – Tarup won 8-4. This took place in the same year after the first main branch of Odense County, following a meeting on coaching with Povl Jør-gensen, decided to set up a committee on ball games, to organize handball in the local branches (*Ungdom og Idræt* 1937/37: 478), and in the same year that VHF staged the first national championship (although only for clubs on the islands).

Mediation

Towards Christmas the same year came the final announcement: the game had developed with such incredible speed that there was hardly a branch where handball was not played. Yet this brought further obligations. If the game was not be coarsened as football had been (*Ungdom og Idræt* 1937/38: 486), there had to be intervention in time, with great responsibility incumbent on the leaders to ensure "ball control" and "good behaviour on the pitch", as Aage Astrup of Odense wrote (*Ungdom og Idræt* 1937/46: 585). The latter point of view is interesting because, more clearly than anything previously heard in the debate, it links character formation and technical skills. There was a movement towards combining sporting skill with education, without abandoning by any means the idealistic purpose. But this was the first serious admission that handball had the potential to achieve this. With this "solution", it was difficult to maintain the harsh dismissal of handball seen in the first years of the 1930s. DDG could keep its profile and simultaneously modernize its content.

In 1939 this dual outlook was summed up in a piece signed A.P.D. (presumably A. Pedersen Dømmestrup), advocating that handball should be pursued like gymnastics: "One can never learn to play handball without thorough instruction, and calm, order, good tone; discipline, in the best sense of the word, are necessary if instruction is to take place" (*Ungdom og Idræt* 1939/23: 303).

With this the Gordian knot seemed to be cut. The common denominator was discipline, understood as a concentration on handball as a special sporting discipline and as a branch of sport that would be characterized by order and orderly behaviour. It was difficult to oppose such an elegant – albeit perhaps rather too metaphorical – mediation. The debate about handball slowly ebbed out during 1939, and it was a stamp of definitive approval that a double course was held at Fuglsø on 12-14 July 1939, one for referees, one for players. The invitation said that the handball camp was "for everyone with the time and inclination to have a three-day holiday, play handball, and swim, and to take part in a couple of festive evenings with folk dancing, singing, and a campfire" (*Ungdom og Idræt* 1939/23: 306). In other words, handball was easily incorporated into the symbolic and practical repertoire of DDG. This was no doubt what Dømmestrup realized back in 1931, when he endorsed Charles Hansen's ideas about including handball on the programme.

Summing up

If we sum up this course of events, an interesting picture emerges that shows how a sport can develop in the course of a decade from virtually nothing to become public property. If we disregard badminton, in which DDG and DDSG&I also showed considerable interest, especially after 1935, no other sport has had a similar breakthrough. This is due not least to the fact that all three main organizations promoted the game. After a certain hesitation, with the gymnastics side fearing competition and being afraid that the purely sport side would gain the upper hand, doubts increasingly disappeared in the course of the 1930s – also because the editor of *Ungdom og Idræt,* A.P. Dømmestrup, quickly conceived an interest in the matter, and together with Killemose from Vallekilde realized the potential of handball. These two men were among the most ardent advocates of the game, since they saw that it posed no basic threat to the foundation of DDG; on the contrary, they saw that it could be a useful addition to the overall work of the organization.

The context

To understand this side of the matter, it is necessary to go back to 1929 and look at the position of shooting and gymnastics at that time. This was in the midst of the great confrontation between marksmen and gymnasts, which culminated in the schism in autumn 1929. It was also in the midst of another upheaval, the breach between the old and the young Denmark and between two different forms and perceptions of the work of popular national enlightenment. Nowhere in the columns of *Ungdom og Idræt* is this expressed more clearly than in Solvejg Bording's article "In This Age" in March 1929. Here we have another key to an understanding of the triumph of handball.

It is a new and refreshing tone we hear here:

> *No one can continue to live on tradition without renewing it himself; our patriotism must also find its renewal in us. And even though it is not expressed in the same way as it was in the past, even though we are perhaps more careful about talking of our feeling of Danishness, of our love of the flag and our native country, we can nevertheless fight for that, perhaps in a more mundane struggle.* (Ungdom og Idræt 1929/12: 102)

The special foundation on which the shooting and gymnastic clubs had grown had now disappeared, she claimed. To begin with, it had too tenuous a connection to mundane everyday life. Secondly, it was too closely connected with gravity, ceremony, and otherworldliness. Instead she stressed the festivity of gathering with friends in pleasant company. We see here the contours, firstly, of a change from sport as an authoritarian educational instrument to a form of social interaction, and secondly of a change from the nineteenth-century ceremonial nationalism with its royal trappings to the democratic welfare nationalism of the inter-war years, and thirdly a change from the subordination of the individual to a combination of collectivity and individuality, with physical *joie de vivre* and bodily experience as the fulcrum.

It was not long before the response came: in a long, vigorous reply, Johan Brydegaard, Ollerup, dismissed this view as bodily fixation and egocentrism (*Ungdom og Idræt* 1929/15: 135 pp.). This, however, led other people to write in defence of Solvejg Bording. Among them was Killemose who, almost certainly acting on the basis of an article by Charles Hansen, realized that something new was coming. His horrific vision is of a state of affairs in which young people's force for renewal has stagnated, and he sees a risk of this in the present situation, in which young people have become tired of twaddle, bickering, self-worship, and bombastic speeches (*Ungdom og Idræt* 1930/23: 244). In a situation like this, fresh blood was needed, and it is probably here that we can find the explanation for Killemose's interest in ball games as a viable course out of the dead water that threatened young people's idealism, while as an experienced schoolteacher he was also prepared to accept a renewal of form and content, so long as the foundation remained sound.

In this connection we cannot ignore the fact that DDG and DDSG&I could kill several birds with the stone of handball. They could satisfy young people's interest in the new competitively geared sports, such as football, and in outdoor life as in the scout movement (*Ungdom og Idræt* 1930/23: 244), while simultaneously being able to turn this interest in the desired direction. They could also compete with the "ball clubs" and the scouts, and they could cater to the interest in a new and more socially oriented attitude to sport, as expressed by young people like Solvejg Bording. As long as gymnastics still held its bastions, however, they were rather hesitant, but when it became increasingly clear from the mid-1930s that élite gymnastics was an obstacle to "national" sports, and that fewer and fewer of those who had attended the drill instructors' courses wanted to act as leaders, preferring to do gymnastics themselves (*Ungdom og Idræt* 1930/23: 244), the attitude changed gradually. Handball appeared to be the universal remedy that would at once maintain tradition and renew it.

The result

Perhaps the clearest indication that new winds were blowing in the countryside is a piece by Kristian Krogshede in the DDSG&I magazine *Dansk Idræt* from 1934. He writes that footballers and handball players must give up the idea that they can stop training in the winter (*Dansk Idræt* 1934/6). There is no mistaking the message: sport has to be a year-round pursuit. Or to put it another way: it must be possible to live a life totally in the world of sport. This brings us back to our starting point, as outlined above: that handball in many ways served to build a bridge between the world of gymnastics and that of football. That it was able to do this was due not least to the fact that handball gained a central position in both DDG and DDSG&I. Handball owes these two national organizations a significant part of the credit for the spread of the game in the inter-war years. As we read in the official statistical reports for 1938:

> The growing interest in handball in recent years has had the effect that handball is by far the most widespread of all the sports that the major gymnastics organizations have adopted alongside gymnastics. (Danmarks Statistik 1938: 318).

There were a total of 28,110 active handball players in 1938. The remarkable thing is that women made up the largest group, with 11,860 active players. Yet it is equally remarkable that just five years later there were as many as 59,000 active handball players (*Dansk Idræts Forbund* ed. 1944/6: 65). This doubling was particularly due to vigorous growth in rural districts, where the national organizations were strongest. In the capital, men predominated, whereas in Jutland there was a significant preponderance of women, among both seniors and juniors.

Conclusion

This chapter has been discussing some of the reasons why handball enjoys a much greater spread in Denmark than in most other countries. On the other hand, that may also be one of the reasons why Denmark did not reach the international élite until relatively late.

It is in fact a rather fascinating story, because, although people were unaware at the time, it has exerted a decisive influence on the conditions in which the sport has been played in Denmark. For the two major gymnastics associations, De Danske Skytte-, Gymnastik-og Idrætsforeninger (DDSG&I, The Danish Shooting, Gymnastics and Athletics Clubs) and De Danske Gymnastikforeninger (DDG, The Danish Gymnastics Clubs), the introduction of handball was essential for survival at a time when support for gymnastics was falling disastrously, and the growing membership of these two organizations in the 1930s was due solely to the incorporation of handball in their sports programmes.

Right from the start, Dansk Håndboll Forbund (The Danish Handball Association), founded in 1935, profited from the spread of handball through the national sports organizations and the YMCA branches, since the number of clubs and individuals from these organizations who joined the Handball Association guaranteed a growth that has no counterpart in any other country.

In the organizations playing handball in Denmark, there has never been any hostility among the handball leaders, unlike the case, say, in Germany before the Nazi take-over in 1933. As a result, all handball players have pulled together, apart from some differences of opinion about the rules in the period 1935-44. The disagreements chiefly concerned internal Danish matters, and also Denmark's relation to other countries. When the Danes discussed the rules of the game, they all sat round the same table, not only the organizations just mentioned but also school sports. In some situations, of course, the willingness to cooperate could not avoid being affected by conflicts of interest, chiefly about deciding the opening and closing dates of the seasons.

SPORT AT THE FRONT: FOOTBALL AND NATION IN FINLAND DURING THE SECOND WORLD WAR

On 12 March 1940 the Winter War between Finland and the Soviet Union came to an end. After a heroic effort, Finland had suffered a painful defeat. Roughly 22,500 Finns lost their lives or were reported missing. In economic terms the war – and the peace treaty – meant that Finland lost 10 per cent of its cultivated land and 11 per cent of its forest, mostly in Karelia. The inhabitants of the territory that had to be ceded left their native districts and headed west. As a result, opportunities for a livelihood had to be created for thousands of evacuees. Finnish society faced hard times, and it was easy to agree with J.L. Runeberg's old statement that "our land is poor and so will remain".

This disheartening situation provoked powerful reactions and revanchist desires, especially among the right-wingers who in the 1930s had expressed hopes of establishing a Greater Finland incorporating areas far into East Karelia on the other side of the border, areas which were perceived as old, "genuine" Finnish, and which were now suffering under Russian – and worse, Soviet – repression. Just as the Civil War in 1918 had been launched as a war of liberation against Russian infringement (Ylikangas 1995) there was now talk of a new war of liberation, this time to reconquer the parts of Karelia that had been lost with the Peace of Moscow that ended the Winter War. And on 26 June 1941 – four days after Germany attacked the Soviet Union – Finland sided with Germany and began what was later to be known as the Continuation War.

Background

The Continuation War can, however, also be seen in a wider perspective, where you can draw lines back into the young Finnish nation's history and into the conflict between the two cultural parts of the population: the Swedish and the Finnish speaking.

This conflict derived partly from Finland's secession from Sweden 1809 with the matching change into the status of an autonomous Grand Duchy under the reign of the Russian czar, partly from the general rise of national awakenings that took place in Europe throughout the first half of 19th century. The relation between these two parts of the population became more and more sinister in the 1840s after the publication of J.V. Snellman's journal *Saima* that normally is held as the first manifestation of a Finnish nationalism – although written in Swedish (Lind 1989: 51). The Finnish speaking population, under the leadership of Fennomans like Snellman, Yrjö-Koskinen and Ahlqvist-Oksanen, was in rising degree to be aware of its own cultural and ethnic peculiarities. Language researchers like M.A. Castrén, folklorists and archeologists concomitantly undertook journeys to Russia and Siberia and tried to prove common traits with Finnish-Ugrian speaking people at other places in the Russian realm. This was intended to be a counterweight to the Swedish and Nordic heritage that was considered to be a hinderness of the wakening of the Finnish people. The turmoil caused by the severe russification policy of Czar Nicolas II and not least the Guvernor-General Bobrikov in the Grand Duchy around the turn of the 1900s diminished the inner-Finnish conflicts, but as this russification after Eugen Schauman's murder of Bobrikov in 1904 was alleviated, time was due for a revitalization of the conflict between the Swedish and the Finnish speaking; this happened not least because of the 1902 language ordinance, which finally fullfilled the promise, made by Czar Alexander II in 1863, to place Finnish on an equal footing with Swedish as part of at "devide-and-rule" policy (Jussila 1999: 67).

The Finnish national independence 1917 did not put an end to the conflict. Just as there were strong Finnish groups that wanted to make a final solution with the "Reds" there were people who took a hard stance against "the Swedes". Not least in parties of the Agrarians and the Conservatives were thoughts of a "Pure-Finnish" policy prevalent. It was championed by the slogan "yksi mieli, yksi kieli" (i.e. one people, one language), dating back to 1860. The radical version of these ideas flourished in the two right wing groupings of AKS, an intellectual students' organisation (Klinge 1988: 289 ff.), and the peasant populist Lapua Movement with its close connections to parts of the Finnish army and the Finnish wood industry. In both movements ideas of a Great Finland were rummaging, according to which Finland should extend its territory eastwards in the wastelands of Karelia, where the population according to

Finnish race- and folklore theories lived and spoke in a Finnish way and consequently were waiting for their Western Finnish brothers to release them. It is in obscure "Pure-Finnish" dreams like these that football at the front during the Second World War should be contextualized.

The Second World War once again provided a good chance of rapprochement between the Swedish and Finnish speaking, as they were exposed to a common danger in their fight against the Russian communists and for the maintenance of Finnish sovereignty. But great politics and "the great history" is one thing; "the small history" and the "banal nationalism" is another thing. Were all Finns eventually willing to acknowledge even the "Reds'" and the "Swedes'" contribution to the defence of the Finnish nation state and to accept their legitimacy as nation defenders on equal terms?

Purpose

To put it in another way, this essay deals with the answer of two questions: 1) Did the Second World War – and the Continuation War in particular – imply a weakening or a strengthening of the Swedish speaking Finns' integration in the Finnish nation? 2) What role did sport play in this possible integration?

No matter what the answers to these questions might be, the purpose is to show that sport always exists in correlation and interplay with the "great history". Sport's history can hardly be written isolatedly, as it is always hegemonically dominated by a history bigger than itself. In this case the history of the survival of the Finnish nation and the integration of a more or less heterogeneous population. On the other hand sport's contribution to the "great history" is also worth considering, as sport as part of society also make an impact on peoples lives and experiences of taking part of the "great history", for instance war. *In casu*: did the Swedish Finns' representation by means of an "innocent" activity as football *per se* facilitate their integration into the Finnish nation? Or did this sport activity need to be flanked by participation of a more severe kind, as for instance heroic national warfare? Or was it eventually this very interplay between war and civic aspirations that turned out to be decisive?

At any rate, war is a bizarre phenomenon. One of the peculiarities of it, often neglected, is that in spite of war, civil life has to continue. Life has to be lived even in wartimes. Concomitantly, babies are born, people fall in love and pass time and leisure activities flourish best they can. People dance, sing, go to the theatre – and play football, even in the shadows of bombing machines.

So, this article examines the sporting aspects of this Continuation War, seeking to shed light on an important phase in the history of Finland in the twentieth century, and to elucidate one aspect of civil life in Finland during the Second World War, namely football, and its relation to the military part of Finland' s history in these years. Which impact did the martial circumstances have on sport? How was it possible to maintain sport activities? What was the relationship between people at the front and civil society during the extraordinary conditions that prevailed all over Scandinavia – and especially in Finland – during the Second World War? Did sport function as a promotor facilitating the contact between different social and cultural parts of Finnish society during these years?

My purpose is, in short, to show that not only the soldiers' fight, but also the civic activities of sport made its contribution to Finnish nationalism, including the acknowledgement of the Swedish speaking part of Finnish civic society and concomitantly the acknowledgement of the Finnish-Swedish as part of the Finnish nation as a whole.

Warfare for what and whom?

The whole of Finnish society was not enthusiastic about the Continuation War. Väinö Linna's world-famous novels are the most precise expression of the scepticism among the privates about the Greater Finnish warfare. This applied to the majority of "Red" Finland, which, as Heikki Ylikangas has shown in such detail, had been crushed by mass executions during the Civil War in 1918 and subsequent internment in prison camps. When the Winter War broke out in 1939, the "Reds" and their successors were not enlisted for purely military operations. They therefore did not have an obvious revanchist motive in 1941, and they can scarcely have felt a strong desire to engage in war against the model Soviet state.

None the less, they were called up to serve in the Continuation War, when every able-bodied man was needed for the ambitious Greater Finnish project of liberation and revenge. This meant that, whereas only about 300,000 soldiers had been drafted for the Winter War, twice as many were called up for the Continuation War (Ylikangas 1995: 478).

Yet there were other forces than socialist and communist workers who were sceptical about the Greater Finnish dreams. This was the case for much of the Swedish-speaking population, especially the farmers and craftsmen who lived up in Ostrobothnia on the west coast. From their point of view, having traditionally always looked towards Sweden and regarded Stockholm in many ways as the relevant metropolis, rather than Helsinki, it seemed mad to start a large-scale campaign far off in Karelia. Despite this they took part, albeit without any great enthusiasm, because they had a feeling that the war had also been provoked by powerful forces in Finnish big business in general, and the forestry industry in particular, which saw the chance of enormous profits from the conquest of large areas of forest to the east (Vehviläinen 1976; Meinander 2001: 117 ff.). The situation was summed up by the sailor and soldier Myra, whom Hilding Nyström quotes in his front-memoirbook *Krigare 1944* ("Warriors 1944"), based on wartime diary notes: "Hey lads, what are we doing here, we Swedish speakers? In the Russian forests! If we were right in the head we wouldn't be involved in a rotten cause." (Nyström 1994: 20).

In sporting circles in Finland there were also divided opinions about participation in the war. In the 1920s and 1930s there had been a considerable amount of sporting activity (shooting, athletics, and skiing) in the right-wing paramilitary Civil Guards (*skyddskårer*), which had played a major part in the murder purges of the Civil War and in the militarization of the Finnish right wing in the first years of the 1930s (Vasara 1995). These Civil Guards, which existed alongside the proper club-organized sport, partly laid the foundation for the good physical condition of the Finnish troops during the Winter War (Römpötti 1995). The people in these circles felt a strong sympathy for Germany.

As a whole, the Finnish sports movement was highly politicized in the inter-war years. Just as many "Reds" were excluded from military service, many were denied admission to the Finnish Gymnastics and Sports Association (SVUL) because they had been on the "Red" side in the Civil War. They therefore founded the Finnish Workers' Sports Federation (TUL) (Hentilä 1982), not just on ideological grounds but also to satisfy their desire to compete in sports. Not surprisingly, this association had a somewhat ambivalent attitude to participation in the war, since they were Soviet-oriented. But they gave in and went to the front in national comradeship.

But what about a non-martial sport activity, like football, that was not politicized in the same degree? What part did that play in the war? And how did it actually become a part of life on the front?

IR 61

It deserves to be pointed out that the war did not just mean death and destruction, and it by no means put a stop to all civic activities, including sporting activity. As an illustration of this we can begin by looking at the situation of one of the most famous Finnish fighting unit during the Second World War which, strangely enough, was also to play a significant role in Finnish sports history in the last years of the Second World War and the ensuing years. I am referring to the famous infantry regiment, IR 61, which merits a brief account in its own right before we look at the sporting aspects. For the time being, sport must take second place here. IR 61's place in Finnish history is not least due to the part played by the regiment in the fighting on the Karelian Isthmus in the time around Midsummer 1944, in connection with the Battle of Tienhaara, which is perceived as one of the most celebrated and heroic of all the Finnish-Russian battles of the entire Second World War

There are several reasons for this fame. To begin with, we must bear in mind that the battle took place in the last spasms of the war, when all the naïve and woolly dreams of a Greater Finland, extending to Far Karelia on the other side of Lake Ladoga, had been crushed, and when desertion had become a serious problem. It was no longer a question of expansion, but of defence. A phase of the war had been reached when it was a matter of saving what could be saved, and now even people who had been opposed to the Continuation War could join in wholeheartedly. In this way the situation was now more reminiscent of the Winter War, whose defensive character made it essentially different from the Continuation War. The situation was that the Soviets were exerting pressure with huge concentrations of troops, with heavy artillery and air support. The idyllic areas on the Isthmus out to the Gulf of Finland, where for centuries Finnish, Swedish, Russian and German citizens had lived together relatively peacefully, where the poet Edith Södergran and the radical cultural circle surrounding the Tulenkantaja group had lived, were lost (Tandefelt 2002; Wahlbeck 1994), the old cosmopolitan city of Viborg on the Karelian Isthmus – Finland's second largest city, just north-west of Leningrad – had fallen, with the citizens evacuated in dramatic circumstances (Lindholm 1995). The Russians were now ready to move forward along the entire south coast of Finland towards Helsinki.

The second reason for the fame of Tienhaara is that the battle was fought with troops who had not been very enthusiastic about the Continuation War, Swedish-speaking soldiers recruited from among the people of Nyland and Åboland in the south and from Ostrobothnia in the north, people who had not felt that the Continuation War was their war. Finland Swedes claimed that it was a premeditated act of the Finnish military leadership, as a prolongation of the Fennicization policy of the 1930s, to deploy the Swedish-speaking troops in the exposed position at Tienhaara. In the official literature on the history of the war, little attention is devoted to Tienhaara, but its position is all the stronger in the folk memory of the Second World War, especially among Swedish speakers.

The third reason for the fame of the battle is probably the one that has meant the most. Here at Tienhaara, more precisely at the little straits of Kivisillansalmi (Stenbrosund), where the Saima Canal leads into the Gulf of Finland and is crossed by the Leningrad–Helsinki railway line, the Finland-Swedish infantry regiment IR 61 dug in, and after inhuman losses – in five or six days of unbroken Soviet infantry and artillery attack with air support – managed to halt the Soviet advance, so that even today Tienhaara is known as "Finland's lock". The bloody battle, which in the course of a week caused about a hundred men each day to die or suffer wounds (losses on the Soviet side were much greater) (Westerlund 1995: 150), is well known to us today thanks to three or four very detailed accounts, based on

diary notes kept by soldiers who took part in and survived the terrible days around Midsummer 1944 (Nykvist 1986; Franzén 1993;
Nyström 1994; Westerlund 1995).

As we have seen, IR 61 was composed of Finland-Swedish units.
Many of the soldiers had fought in the Winter War, but in the summer of 1944 the regiment itself had only been at the front for three
years, having been formed in the summer of 1941. As a consequence,
it had also been at the section of the front in Far Karelia north and
east of Ladoga, and here it had advanced as far as Onega, where it
had suffered considerable losses on the "Svir Front".

The time in east Karelia, however, did not involve constant war.
Much of the day was spent building and fortifying the positions – to
the soldiers' great chagrin, since it meant endless toil, which many
of them perceived as sheer military discipline for its own sake. But
there was also time for other activities, including sports. Shooting
contests were particularly popular, and football and athletic events
were held as well (Franzén 1993: 204).

These sporting activities would indirectly resound all over Finland. The fact was that the Ostrobothnian part of IR 61 included
some troops who were enthusiastic football players who had played
as civilians for the club IFK Vasa in the Finnish first division. This
club is one of the oldest and proudest in Finland.

IFK Vasa

IFK Vasa was founded on 19 September 1900 by secondary school
pupils at the Swedish high school in Vasa, with Harry Schauman
as the driving force. Harry Schauman, incidentally, was related to
Eugen Schauman, the man who in 1904 assassinated the Russian
governor in Finland, Bobrikov, and who had taken part in the Schauman family festivities in Vasa in the 1890s (Wikman 1963: 55 f.).
Before this he had made his first trip to Stockholm on his own, and
it was probably as a result of his frequent contacts with Sweden that
he was seized by an interest in sports in 1900. He was inspired by
the cultivation of youth that was so strong in Sweden in these years
(Berggren 1995), and by the Olympic idealism of Coubertin – despite
the fact that he did not exactly have the body of a sportsman, being
heavy and stocky (Wikman 1963: 40 ff.).

The triggering factor was the foundation of a new sports movement in Sweden in 1895, when a number of young high school
pupils at Norra Real in Stockholm, under the leadership of Louis
Zettersten, decided to form a sports club which would pursue athletics, social activities, and excursions. This was after they had started
to publish *Kamrat-tidningen* ("The Comrade Magazine") in 1893 as
part of the idealistic, liberal and patriotic "Comrade Movement".
The next result was the sports club IFK (Idrottsföreningen Kamraterna, "The Comrades Sports Association"). IFK Stockholm was
the first club belonging to the Comrade Movement to have sports
on the programme, but others quickly followed, in places like Luleå,
Jönköping, and Göteborg, where the famous IFK Göteborg was also
founded in that year, although it did not get going seriously until
1897 (Idrottsföreningen Kamraterna 1995), and in towns such as
Sundsvall and Halmstad, in the latter case with the young Ernst
Wigforss, who would later be Swedish Minister of Finance and one
of the main architects of the Swedish welfare state, as a member
from 1895, when he was only 14 years old (Hallands Idrottsförbund
1993: 54).

Thanks to an announcement in *Kamrat-tidningen*, which was also
read in the Swedish-speaking parts of Finland, the desire to start
sports clubs started in Finland too, first in Uleåborg but later also
in Helsinki, where the enterprising Uno Westerholm – the father
of Finland-Swedish sport – was the driving force. In autumn 1899
he arranged the first club competitions in IFK Helsinki, held in
Kajsaniemi Park in the centre of the city (Björkman 1995: 109). All
in all, the Finnish IFK-movement typically is a part of the Swedish
heritage that many right wing radicals in Finland tried to neglect.

Harry Schauman up in Vasa likewise developed an interest
in sport after the high school in Vasa had formed a "comrades'
club" in 1896, although not at first with sports on the programme.
This only came when Schauman conceived an interest in bringing
together the schoolboys' unorganized sporting activities – running,
high jump, shot-put, and skiing – in proper club form with the
foundation of IFK Vasa (Wikman 1963: 40). By 1901 the IFK Vasa
programme included athletics, cycling, and tennis in the summer,
and skiing and skating in the winter. In a notice printed during the
first year of the magazine *Finsk Idrottsblad* (1904), a writer with the

pen-name H. S-n. mentions that "IFK is the club most in keeping with the times" and that "The interest in physical exercise is steadily increasing in our town" (Finsk Idrottsblad 1904: 11). In 1907 football was added to the activities, with the holding of the first football tournament in Vasa. In the same year, however, IFK Vasa was divided when a number of older members broke away to form the Vasa Sports Society (Vasa Idrottssällskap, VIS). The reason for this is obscure, but according to the VIS jubilee publication in 1937, one factor was that the young people in IFK were just as interested in dancing, amateur drama, and social activities as in sport (Finne 1937: 31), and those interested primarily in sport felt a need for a club of their own. In the next couple of decades IFK and VIS were tough rivals, until they agreed in 1929 to divide up the activities between themselves, so that VIS took charge of gymnastics, athletics, skiing, and other activities, while IFK specialized in football in the summer and bandy in the winter (Lindén 1985: 23).

For IFK this was the starting signal for a relatively quick advancement to the top of Finnish football in the 1930s, when the Finnish Football Association decided in 1930 to expand the existing cup system with a league. Through this IFK Vasa qualified to the first division in 1934 – together with the town's first Finnish-speaking sports club, Vaasan Palloseura (VPS). The first Vasa players on the national team thereby emerged as well, with Lasse "Gandhi" Nordlund being the club's first member to play for Finland's B team in an international against Estonia, while Erik Beijar made his debut for the A team in 1939 in a match against Latvia (Hagman 1985: 48). IFK Vasa had gained its place on the map of Finnish football – and then came the war.

IR 61 and IFK Vasa – a successful couple

The Continuation War, which broke out in the summer of 1941, meant that only eleven rounds of the football tournament could be played that year. After that, everything collapsed. The players had to go the front.

For many of the IFK men this meant serving in the Swedish-speaking regiment IR 61, more specifically its mortar company, which was put together in Vasa and which mainly consisted of men

from that town, including numerous IFK members. The company
was led by Georg Braxén, reserve goalkeeper on IFK's first team.
What could have been more natural than to start at once to put
together a provisional team? They trained in unorganized form
among themselves and with other groups in the company.

IR 61 was first deployed in the coastal defence of East Nyland,
that is, between Helsinki and the Russian border, but in summer
1942 they were moved to the Svir Front in Far Karelia. Some of the
older IFK soldiers had now been sent home, but new ones arrived,
so that the IR 61's regimental football team was composed of a core
of nine first-team players from IFK Vasa. In between the dangerous
patrolling and the regular combat engagement there were opportunities to play football in nearby meadows (Haldin 1985: 93 pp.).
These opportunities did not diminish when yet another IFK man,
"Muffa" Hellström, was appointed IR 61's sports officer. In this
capacity he had a camp for the regiment's footballing élite placed in
the little village of Podporosje, about 10-15 kilometres behind the
front. Most of the best IFK players, and numerous other men, were
sent there for periods. Here, at a good distance from the excitement
of the front, they were kept busy building shelters, working with
telephone and electricity posts and the like, but they were also able
to practise football when the compulsory tasks were over. In this
way a more or less unorganized training camp arose here, where the
men played football virtually every day.

In the summer of 1942 a proper football tournament was arranged for the units of the 17th division, to which IR 61 belonged.
A total of five teams were allowed to play against each other. The
last, decisive match was between IR 61/IFK Vasa and the Hammaren
section, which was mostly recruited from GBK in Gamla Karleby, a
club that was normally no opposition for IFK. This time things went
wrong, however: the evening before the match, the GBK players
invited IFK to a comradely party where they were offered drinks
that were not part of the ordinary fare of the front. This included the
well-known drink "forest rustle". IFK gladly accepted the offer, but
the cunning GBK men made sure to stay off the "rustle" and drink
water instead. The result the next day was an ignominious defeat
at the hands of Hammaren/GBK, otherwise the worst team in the
tournament. IR 61/IFK had to be content with a bronze medal.

Summer of 1943 was also spent on the Svir Front, in circumstances similar to those the year before. The unorganized training camp likewise continued, now that the front had become a quiet position war, although not without danger. The same applied to the 17th division's football tournament, when IR 61/IFK avoided the "forest rustle" and won the tournament hands down. As a reward for this they were allowed to go back on leave to Vasa and organized sport, and here they suffered their only defeat of the season to the IFK players who had stayed at home.

In 1943 the Finnish Football Association tried to resume the league tournament. This had been inactive since 1941, but in the spring of that year IFK had qualified to the first division by wining the second division. The Football Association agreed with the Workers' Sports Federation to have a joint championship series. The Football Association requested leave for the players stationed at various places on the front. For the three rounds they managed to play, IFK Vasa was to bring home five players from the front, whose train journeys had to be coordinated. This was successfully managed, and IFK won two of its matches and drew one. The latter was played against IFK Helsinki in the stadium in the capital, but it was interrupted by an air raid sirene. The unorganized training at the front had stood up to its test, but the tournament was not completed, so IFK were unable to savour the complete triumph.

Other successes awaited them, however, although it took time. The end of the Continuation War put a stop to all further sport in 1944. It was not until the spring of 1945 that the remaining matches of the 1943-44 season could be played. These were also won by IFK Vasa, who were then ready for the final, where they beat TPS Åbo by a resounding 5-1. Of the IFK players, seven had been on the Svir Front and played football together in IR 61.

In the same year – 1945 – the "normal" league championship should have been contested, but it now took the form of a cup series. Here, however, TPS took revenge over IFK with a 2-1 victory. Yet IFK Vasa got its own back in 1945, when as many as six of their players represented Finland, although Sweden easily won the two internationals that were played.

In the next three or four years IFK Vasa continued where they had left off, with the team that was still built up around the Svir

Front core. In 1948 they won their fourth championship since 1943-44, the last three consecutively (they failed only in the 1945 cup), and in 1947 eight IFK players played for the national team at least once. Finnish football had not seen such an achievement since HJK Helsinki in 1917-19 had won the championship three years in a row, when it had moreover been a cup tournament.

When one considers that the Finnish daily press was concordant in its evaluation of the achievements of the national team, that its prime quality was its striking homogeneity, it is not hard to find the reason in the informal but intensive training that took place on the Svir Front, with tough fitness training and exercises in technique, along with the development of a strong team spirit resulting from spending several years together in situations that were, to say the least, stressful. However paradoxical it might sound, it was precisely the extraordinary circumstances that caused this team from Vasa to form a unit that remained strong when there was a return to fairly normalized football after the end of the Continuation War in autumn 1944.

Sport and nation building

From a Finnish point of view, the history of IFK Vasa and IR 61 is both significant in itself and indicative of a more general development. For it marks an important step in the history of sport and for the nation alike. Until the Winter War, Finnish society in general, and Finnish sport in particular, were seriously divided. The wounds from the Civil War were still open. This is connected with the distinctive conditions for nation building in Finland, to which sport also contributed.

The Olympic Games in Stockholm in 1912 played a particularly crucial role for Finnish national self-awareness. Finland was permitted to send independent representatives, even though the country was still part of the Russian Empire. On the procession into Stockholm Stadium, the Finnish team marched behind a sign saying "Finland" and the banner of the Gymnastics Association in Helsinki, although this was removed on the order of the leader of the Russian troop – not least because the Swedish spectators had so vigorously applaudded the entry of the Finnish troop, especially when the stadium band joined in with a tune from Finland, *Björneborgarnas marsch*. This was an epoch-making symbolic representation that was to be of great significance for Finnish nationalism. Finland was well on the way to being placed as an independent country on the world map.

All the greater was the shock caused by the Civil War in 1918. No sooner had the longed-for independence come in 1917 than the internal divisions erupted. The shock had an extraordinary effect because the Finnish national upbringing, which had largely been in the charge of the intellectuals, had so strongly emphasized the national community. This was also true of some intellectual theorists of sport, such as Lauri Pihkala and Artur Eklund, a close friend of Harry Schauman, who stressed sport as an exponent of national strength in his book *Idrottens filosofi* ("The Philosophy of Sport", 1917) (Eklund 1970: 124 ff.).

As has been pointed out (Alapuro 1987; Stenius 1992), the grand lines in the history of Finnish intellectuals have been state-oriented and populist, in that it was an important task for Finnish intellectuals to represent the people *vis-à-vis* the authorities, and also to educate and enlighten the same people. The intellectuals were supposed to listen to the voice of the people and formulate it in public, but simultaneously to ensure that they qualified this voice. In other words, their central task was to act as mediators between the people and the state, with Fennomania as the ideological fulcrum. Sport was perceived as an eminently suitable instrument for this, and Harry Schauman's idealistic initiative should also be seen in the light of these ambitions.

But one thing is an idealistic young person's dreams. Another thing is the hard stuff of social and cultural tensions – and war.

National levelling

Erkki Vasara has analysed how "red" sportsmen in the between war period were excluded from the Finnish Gymnastics and Sports Association (SVUL) and therefore had to found their own Finnish Workers' Sports Federation (TUL). This division did not start to break down until the Winter War and the Continuation War (Vasara 1992). Here Finnish socialist workers also paid their fee for

the survival of the Finnish nation with a growing national respect-
ability as a result.

It has also been pointed out that life on the front led to a level-
ling of the Finnish dialects (Huldén 1980: 294), and the encounter
of different social classes likewise led to a gradual blurring of class
divisions. Nationalism proved here, as so often before, that it was
stronger than all the political isms. The sporting conflict between the
SVUL and the TUL was also mollified, since the sporting activities
that took place on the front took no regard for political oppositions.
In addition, the army leaders took a highly benevolent view of sport
as a way to counteract the dreariness and boredom – and the endless card playing. Sport – as another shared practice alongside the
actual fighting – thereby served as a national cement, bridging the
otherwise violent conflicts of class and language.

In this light, the victorious run of IFK Vasa on the playing field
helped to reinforce the respect that IR 61 created for the Finland-
Swedes at Tienhaara. Tienhaara showed that, when it came to the
shared national cause, the Finland-Swedes were just as good Finland-
ers as the Finnish-speakers. IFK Vasa's championships underlined
this.

As a concluding remark it can be pointed out that this study
shows one example of how the war influenced civil society as can be
seen in the case of football; but it is also evident that civil activities
such as football as well had a certain impact of how warfare was
experienced. The civic nationalism of football made it own contribution to the more heroic part of the war and moreover functioned
as a mediator between the front and life at home – and, not least,
as a mediator between the cultural and linguistic different parts of
Finnish society. Not just heroic warfare but also civic activities like
football promoted the conspicuous but also conciliatory revitalization of nation building in Finland during the war which after
decades of mistrust eventually ended the cultural fight between the
Swedish and the Finnish speaking part of society.

SPORT AND SPACE IN THE NORDIC WORLD

There is solid evidence to suggest that the excellent sports facilities to be found in the Nordic countries have enhanced participation in sport: The greater the number of sports facilities available, the greater the number of participants. It seems clear also that those clubs with older grounds and pitches have had advantages over those that lacked these amenities. The availability of sport space seems to be crucial for the diffusion of sport, as can be demonstrated, for instance, by the history of badminton in Denmark and ice hockey in Sweden and Finland. In short, sport demands space, but the facilities create sport.

However, the question of sport facilities has almost been totally neglected in the sports history of Norden. Only a few books and articles have paid attention to this problem and so far no research has dealt with this issue on a Nordic level *in toto*. This is unsatisfactory because, on the one hand, the question of facilities seems to be a crucial part of the development of sports and leisure history and, on the other hand, seems to provide one way of pointing out the connections between sport and local society.

So, this article aims at providing a survey of the historical development of sport facilities in the Nordic countries with the intention of presenting a *vue* over the various stages in this development. This implies that the intention is more synthetic than analytical and more occupied with the construction of a research area for the future than with critique. The idea argued is that, on the whole, Nordic sport facilities are characterized by a move from a multifunctional to a mono-functional space used only by and for sport. In other words, the provision of such separated sport places is evidence of the institutionalization of sport as a distinct and discriminate part of society. But the provision of sports facilities has also functioned as a contribution to the development of a special local identity and pride, as can be demonstrated by the example of Halmstad.

and litheness (Olsson 1983). Games with sticks and wooden pins existed here as in the rest of the heavily wooded Nordic countries. A game, which consisted of rolling a section of a tree trunk on a track between two opposing teams, also existed in those parts of the Nordic countries where towns or groups of farms lay close together, as in Fyn and Sjælland, Dalarna and Ostrobothnia.

Games and play did not have any designated space. They took place where it was easiest: in meadows, hay fields, streets and squares. Nordic 'pre-sport' had to fit in with work and accommodate to the struggle for daily bread that dominated life (Gaunt 1983). It could be difficult to decide when work stopped and games and play started.

In this 'pre-sport' era – the first, and the longest, period in the history of sport in the Nordic countries – sport did not have its own space. The space for sport was neither permanent nor demarcated, there was no clear distinction between participant and spectator, and in practise often all those present could be participants. This period was only gradually phased out, and reminiscences of it could still be recorded as late as in the 1950s (Kayser Nielsen 1995a).

Formal space for sport existed in neither rural nor in urban culture. As Henrik Stenius has pointed out, in Helsinki, as late as 1875, there was an indistinct "drawing of borders between amusement, educational distraction and charity" (Stenius 1981: 63). At the popular festivals that took place from the mid-nineteenth century in Åbo, Helsinki and Viborg, the programme included various competitions such as sack-races, bag punching, climbing, shooting, swinging and music and singing (Björkman 1987: 29). The boundary between circus, acrobatics, popular outings and sport could at this time, and indeed up to the First World War, be very difficult to draw (Laine 1992): It is not clear if the Brunnspark and Kaisaniemi Park in the middle of Helsinki were first and foremost sports grounds, amusement parks or recreational areas. This confusion still exists: public activities in stadiums can even nowadays embrace the characteristics of circus, carnival and sport (Kayser Nielsen 1995e).

Separation between sportsmen and spectators
The end of the eighteenth century brought the first changes to the 'pre-sport' pattern. Formalized and systematic sport gradually

emerged. In Denmark in about 1790 the brothers C.D. and J.L. Reventlow, inspired by the new European philanthropic ideas, started gymnastics exercises in the schools on their properties for farmers' children, and in Copenhagen, shortly after 1800, Nachtegall initiated swimming for naval midshipmen in Copenhagen harbour, as can be seen elsewhere in this book. In Sweden, in 1796, the mathematics professor, Jöns Svanberg, started the Uppsala *Simsällskap* (Uppsala Swimming Club), considered to be the world's oldest sports club (Moen 1992: 60).

A lack of proper and adequate facilities was typical: in Uppsala they swam in the river Fyrisån south of the town, and in Copenhagen mostly in the harbour at Gammelholm. For races there were no purpose-built pool facilities, even though there were competitions. This state of affairs continued into the twentieth century: For instance in the 1930s in Norrnäs, in Ostrobothnia, the local youth association arranged swimming competitions at Nissasgrund out in the archipelago (Finell 1995: 136). It is doubtful if there were proper, i.e. regular sport competitions in this second stage. However, one important matter was settled: the distinction between the sportsman and the spectator was increasingly made. Contrary to the past agrarian custom, people either participated or watched.

From the last quarter of the nineteenth century this division between performer and spectator was most marked in indoor winter voluntary gymnastics. In Finland they practised in school gymnasiums (in the towns) or in the youth associations' clubs (in the countryside). In the village halls that sprang up after 1880 in Denmark, inspired by the Grundtvigian movement, there were simply no spectators. Gymnastics took place behind closed doors, although an exception was made for the performance at Easter time when the public was invited. Consequently, it can be maintained that Grundtvigian gymnastics in Denmark had incidentally had a strong influence on the modernization of sport and the demise of rural recreation (Kayser Nielsen 1993/94).

Space, time, rules and equipment were all affected by the emerging division between performer and spectator. The early rowing competitions in Bergen were typical. They lay on the border between 'pre-sport' and sports (Goksøyr 1990). Here there were neither fixed nor permanent facilities, and as with the 'pre-modern' sports play and games it was more a question of winning over each other than of relating to an abstract record. Neither time nor space were decisive factors. But, gradually, it became important not only to win against the other competitors but also to win in an excellent time. And the excellence of this time could only be acknowledged in a space used only for sport without disturbance from non-sportsmen.

Even today, to an extent, we are still in the pre-Cartesian world, where circumstances in some fields play a decisive role. The sports world is neither timeless, universal, nor general – only the sport activities are. Local, specific and time-specific conditions still characterize sports which still have not been fully decontextualized, provided that sport is seen in its context.

In the nineteenth century decontextualizing, involving separation between performer and spectator, could be a lengthy process, as can be seen from an example shortly before 1914, when a football competition in Aars in North Jutland was suddenly stopped by a group of sober churchgoer's wandering along a path right across the pitch (Samuelsen 1983: 23). On the island of Bornholm it was said of the beginning of a football match in Aarsballe in 1909: "The first Sunday when there was a game, colourful poles were set up for the goal with a cow tether across the top. Everyone from Aarsballe and all the male football-fans from the neighbourhood had got together – and there were many who, in their excitement, threw themselves into the play with the round leather ball" (BBU 1957: 32). To keep participants and spectators separated was apparently a difficult task.

From multi- to mono-functional space for sport

Until 1900 space for sport, still not decontextualized, still not separated from the spectator, and still not detached from specific local conditions, was not yet mono-functional. The struggle for mono-functional space for sports characterizes the third stage of the evolution of sports space. It covers roughly the first half of the twentieth century.

In Borås the first trotting race was held in 1885 on the ice of Lake Tolken, which had been used the year before for a sledding competition (Segerblom 1986: 12). The tendency here, as in so many other towns, was towards establishing a facility only for sports, and preferably only for one form of sport. In contrast multi-functional space for sport characterized the ad hoc sports sites on the farmers' fields, which were used in and around many country towns in all Nordic countries until about 1960: each year sportsmen rented the best possible place for a summer, either in exchange for a box of cigars or for a sum of money.

In the village of Klokkerholm, in Vendsyssel in Northern Denmark, the sports clubs rented a field on the condition that cows did not graze there. In the same place in 1934 a farmer sought compensation for grain ruined by the sports club: when the ball was kicked into his grain fields, the grain was trampled down (Kayser Nielsen 1994a). On Bornholm in the inter-war years Arnakke's dependency on sheep breeding and grain growing meant that teams had to play alternatively on an area first to the south of, and then to the north of Sdr. Landevej (lit. South Road). Earlier they had to burn away the heather with petroleum and clear stones from the tracks (BBU 1957: 34). There were constant conflicts.

The village of Trelde in East Jutland provides evidence of a characteristic Danish progression in the third stage of sport space. It has four parts. First, in the 1930s there were no fixed places to play. Pitches were borrowed or rented – as in Klokkerholm and a number of other towns – preferably from sports-loving farmers. It was necessary, if troublesome, to first remove the dung from the ground. Despite the less than ideal conditions, permanent use of the site could never be guaranteed. Access was arranged from year to year. Then in the early 1940s the parish council rented out specified sports grounds in the summer. Pitches continued to change from year by year, but matters had improved. Continuity was assured. In addition the Council assumed responsibility for the upkeep of the fields. In 1948 sports grounds for the first time became permanent in the form of a designated ground in two of the parish's three villages: Trelde and Egeskov. Finally in 1954 a large comprehensive sports facility was constructed around the new, big municipal community building in Bøgeskov in the middle of the parish (Kayser Nielsen 1995c). With this innovation, space for sports entered its fourth stage of permanency, standardization and mono-functionalism.

Around 1920 in Närpes in western Finland, sports activities

started on what was called Ryssbacken (lit. "The Russian hill", named after a prison camp for the "Reds" after the end of the Civil War 1917-18). The highway was used as a running track by the athletes. A regular sports facility thus came into being during the 1920s, and by 1931 in Skarpängen by the Närpes river, a large athletics ground was constructed on a voluntary basis, but with help from the municipality (compare the introduction of Halmstad). During the 1980s another new large facility was added, and in the 1990s an ice hockey hall (Böling 1986).

What these various efforts to establish space for sport illustrate is that in the Nordic countries voluntary action has played an important part in the creation of sports space, but in Finland and Sweden local authorities in the countryside have supported the establishment of sports facilities earlier and more actively than in Denmark where the rural parish councils and the smaller urban councils were quite tight-fisted all through the inter-war years. In Norway the sports clubs and the public each owned about 40% of the sports facilities, while private and other organizations owned and ran the remaining 20% (Loland 1995: 256). Finland and Sweden thus constitute one extreme, Norway another, while Denmark takes up the middle ground.

Permanent mono-functional space for sport

While permanent, standardized sports facilities in the Nordic countryside were, as a rule, first acquired after the Second World War, they could already be seen in many towns following the First World War. Kolding in South-East Jutland illustrates this well: The Kolding Cricket Club, founded in 1867, had to use the town market place at the end of Låsbygade. Here, the cricket pitch was not only situated on a knoll that sloped steeply and unevenly, but the players could never be sure that it was available as the municipality rented it out for other activities also. Fortunately, however, Kolding in quite a roundabout way gradually acquired independent sports facilities and a stadium for the whole town (Sørensen 1979).

A first step was taken when in 1896 the Kolding Cycle Club planned a cycle track, "as all the other big cities have". Together with the town's other cycle club, "Old Boys", they wanted to build a facility that could be used as an ice- rink in the winter. A joint-venture company, "Kolding Cycle-, Ice- and Sportsground" was established and a track was constructed in 1898 in the north-western part of the town with a stately pavilion, Olympia. However, the enterprise lost money and in 1900 the town council bought the facility. The bicycle club collapsed, but it had nevertheless succeeded in creating the biggest sports facility in the town. In the years to come this was to accommodate most outdoor sports in Kolding, partly because the space was rented out to Kolding Idrætsforening (The Kolding Sports Club). In the long run the facilities were not considered suitable for sport, because the field was also used for cattle shows. Kolding municipality tried to improve the pitches, but had finally to give up, and in 1927 the town council decided to build a completely new facility nearby with some financial assistance from local sportsmen. In 1931 the facility was ready. In 1933 many training pitches were added. Local opinion was unanimous: the town now had the country's most beautiful and best facility. For the first time Kolding had a mono-functional facility to be used for sport and only for sport. Space for sport had entered its fourth and final stage in Kolding.

In the construction of Aarhus Stadium (Denmark) in the years 1918-20 there was similar cooperation between the private and the public sector. The initiative was taken by the sports clubs. A number of clubs had tried to persuade the town council to support a bigger sports ground, but their efforts were not successful, as they could not all agree on a common representative to approach the municipality. It was not until well-known sportsmen turned to Frederik Lausen, a director of Aarhus Oliefabrik, a local industrial company, that things started to happen. Lausen was a successful industrialist with many irons in the fire and contributed financially to the stadium project. His connections with other well- known citizens ensured further donations. Simultaneously he reorganized the sports clubs, so that with a common board they could represent sportsmen in the stadium project. All this bore fruit as the town council promised the necessary ground and provided an access road. Financially, the enterprise was an enormous challenge. The cost was estimated at 230,000 DKK, but the actual cost of the stadium was 430,000 DKK. Eventually private contributions covered about 380,000 DKK and the town council gave 280,000 DKK. On top of this, the state pro-

reflected social idealism and mono-functionalism; the new halls of
the 1980s and 1990s are apparently oriented more towards multi-
functionalism, entrepreneurship and profit. The Nordic nations
have travelled a long way from the colourful national romanticism
around 1900, when the big moat at the Castle in Varberg was used
as a showplace for amateur gymnastics and athletics, and the first
official football match in the town was played on Children's Day in
1906 (Hallands Bollförbund 1993: 34).

Centralizing the space for sports

The implacable shift to an increasing mono-functionalism of sport
space was complemented by a corresponding concern to concentrate. Examples of this are legion. Take one example only – Vasa
in Finland. In the southern part of the city, around the eastward
motorway, gathered together are the town's stadium, tennis and
squash facilities, ice hockey hall, swimming pool, trotting track,
football track and the *pesäpallo* (Finnish ball game resembling
baseball). Sports organizations and the municipality have always
disagreed about control. The first disagreements go back to 1919
(Finne 1937: 43). In both the 1950s and 1960s the situation became
more aggravated. During both decades the municipality laid claims
to the area for road-building, and IFK Vasa had time and again to
see its track facilities destroyed. Nevertheless, despite these conflicts
the municipality has continued to support centralization with only
the occasional self-interested heretical deviation.

Concentrations like Vasa are commonplace in the Nordic communities. In numerous other Finnish towns, such as Alajärvi and
Kauhajoki, the same pattern can be seen as in Borås and Uppsala in
Sweden (Moen 1992: 93). Aarhus provides a Danish example (many
others could be provided). Here, next to the stadium, two halls,
an outdoor training track, a bicycle and a trotting track, as well as
a badminton hall are located. In addition, a new large sports hall
was built in 2003 in connection with the modernization of Aarhus
Stadium; the whole complex has been bestowed the pompous name
"Athletion". This tendency to centralization is not new and should
be seen as directly linked to cost. The different town councils have
chosen to geographically concentrate the facilities for which they

are responsible. This in turn has meant, for example, dispensing with sports facilities that were in the way of town development (Lund 1993: 108) as well as profitable industrial and commercial initiatives. In Gothenburg in 1923, the town administration sacrificed the prestigious sports facility, Walhalla, where the Örgryte club had its facilities (Persson 1994).

However, it is in Gothenburg that centralization has met with determined – if rare – opposition. All through the 1980s the three big football clubs in Gothenburg shared the 50,000 seat capacity Nya Ullevi stadium, erected in connection with the FIFA World Cup in football in 1958. It was also used, however, for speedway, opera and rock concerts (Moen 1995: 204). In the 1990s the clubs went back to the smaller and intimate Gamla Ullevi with its wooden platforms and close proximity between spectators and players (Lindberg 1994: 258). This was the city's traditional stadium, where the clubs felt part of tradition and in control of their own affairs and where the spectators and supporters were able to regain a sense of identity (Samuelsson 1995). Many stories are told about the Gamla Ullevi, which illustrate the transformation of action into meaningful experience. In effect the clubs re-"invented traditions" through sport space in a period of modernization, centralization and commercialism.

Facilities as sport promotor

The history of the space for sport is concerned with the extent to which this space has played a part in the popularization of sport. Clothes make people, it is said, and likewise participation in sport, it can be asserted, has shown itself to be greatly determined both by the peculiarities of landscape and the presence of good facilities.

In Oslo the Arbeidernes Idrettsforbund (Working Mens' Sports Association) complained during the inter-war years that the poorer, eastern, part of Oslo, where the league had most support, was treated unfairly in respect to the provision of facilities in comparison with richer western Oslo, with the result that the Oslo workers did not have the same chances of sporting success (Hodne 1995: 149). In Hvide Sande on the west coast of Jutland, badminton was taken seriously only after a hall had been erected in Hvide Sande in 1972. In Helsinki, Helsingfors Gymnastikklubb was in the school Normallyceet ("Norsen"), where the gymnasts met from 1880-1930. Consequently many members of the club's leadership were former pupils of the school. Even after the club moved to its own premises on Lilla Robertsgatan in 1930, the history of the club was influenced by its first location (Meinander 1996: 19). The adequacy of the provision of space for sport will now be considered in connection with the diffusion of handball, badminton and ice hockey.

Team handball

Team handball began as an indoor game in the Nordic countries. In many cities, however, there was great difficulty in finding a large enough hall. It is hardly a coincidence, therefore, that the early development and expansion of team handball was greatest in the cities where there was easy access to adequate space, as in capital cities and garrison towns such as Viborg and Fredericia in Denmark and Karlskrona in Sweden. All are, or have been, great handball towns. Handball flourished also in other cities that had an appropriate hall available. In Gothenburg in the 1920s handball gained foot, not least due to the ready access to Navy and Army facilities (Persson 1997), and later the Mässhall at the Heden-field, for example, proved very suitable (Olsson 1991). In Kolding, the so-called "Belgian halls" dating from the German occupation during the Second World War played a decisive role in the expansion of handball and, eventually, in the success of team handball in Kolding Idrætsforening (Kolding Sports Club).

However the limited general availability of halls during the inter-war years obviously meant that the game could only expand slowly in the Nordic towns and villages. An important step forward was first taken in the Danish countryside when the "Folk High Schools" took up the game. At Ollerup Gymnastikhøjskole (Ollerup Gymnastics Academy), for example, gymnastic instructors attended "platoon commander" training, which included handball, and took the game back to the parishes where it then developed rapidly as an outdoor rather than indoor sport. At that time when there were no designated sport spaces and sportsmen had to plead to the farmers for a field to rent for sport, it was easier to find space for a small handball court than it was to find space for a large football pitch.

In the interwar period handball proved an asset to sport and sports clubs, because during the winter months gymnastics were not enough to keep the clubs going. But thanks to the diffusion of handball and badminton the clubs picked up. It was women who first took to handball (in many places men considered it to be a "girls' game"). To make it possible to play handball, many of the girls employed as maids had a clause written into their contract stating that their work day should finish at 8 p.m. Thus, males played football, and females played handball in the evenings – a useful arrangement for socializing. One by-product was an increasing fraternization between the sexes, which meant that young men – as in the village of Mønsted (Denmark), for example – no longer needed to peep through a keyhole during gymnastics training for a glimpse of a leg or a stocking (Gjøde Nielsen 1994: 102) but could view "the splendour" openly on training evenings!

As the sports world became "eroticized", and both sexes engaged in sport during summer and winter, "sport parties" developed in the 1930s. Neighbouring clubs – or even those further afield – were invited to a gathering on Sundays, followed by dancing in the evening. They were a great success: the clubs' finances improved, the "sweetheart market" increased, space for sport increased, the number of sportsmen and -women increased, and "sport marriages" increased.

Badminton

Local spatial conditions were also important to the diffusion of badminton. Up until the First World War the game had rarely been played in the Nordic countries, and then mostly on estates with English connections. Matters improved when, at the beginning of the 1920s, Skovshoved Badminton Club in Copenhagen bought a former barracks as a club house. Other clubs were also established, but had to make do with playing badminton in the gymnastic halls of schools. One of the players from Skovshoved came from the little town of Stubbekøbing on the island of Falster. He introduced the game there, and it became so popular that the new badminton club soon had sixty active members. In Stubbekøbing, however, lack of space meant that "singles" could hardly be allowed, so Stubbekøbing players were known "doubles" specialists! Special local conditions influenced play in other places, too. In 1935 Gentofte Badminton Klub from Copenhagen went on tour to Fyn to enhance the awareness of the game. In Aarup, as in other places, they had to play in schools and halls with low ceilings and found that the Aarup players did not hit "clears", but had developed brilliant "drop shots" and "drives"!

Despite poor facilities in many places, the game of badminton became very popular during the 1930s. The game was easy, and above needed little space. It could be played in gymnastic halls, hotel dance halls and assembly halls – and in fact an important explanation for the international success of Danish badminton could be in the availability of facilities as almost every parish had either a gymnastics hall or an assembly hall. Investigations show that the availability of space in which to play the game is a far more plausible reason for its popularity than speculative biological or socio-psychological theories.

Ice hockey

The availability of playing space also affected the spread of ice hockey. Climatic conditions for the game are in themselves good in the Nordic countries with a landscape of many lakes, creeks and frosty winters, but dependence on often unsafe outdoor facilities was not really satisfactory. Before the Second World War outdoor ice hockey was played in Copenhagen, and was also played after the war in a number of towns in Jutland: Esbjerg, Silkeborg and Horsens. In Horsens a cold-store by the harbour was used for some time, but proved insufficient. However, despite a keen spectator interest – in 1947 a spectator in Horsens said in his enthusiasm: "I wish I could stay here – and not have to go and preach" (*Horsens Avis* 13th January 1947) – the game declined. The players had to train and play their "home" matches either in Esbjerg, Vojens or Aarhus, so in spite of talent the game in Horsens eventually died out due to a lack of adequate facilities. The municipality favoured football and had no real interest in the provision of an ice hockey stadium (Kayser Nielsen 1998b). In Esbjerg, for example, the situation was different. The local authorities supported the sport and it survived,

also because the chairman of the ice hockey club fought stubbornly
– first for an outdoor rink, and then for a covered rink (Grinderslev
1998). Consequently, Esbjerg became one of the leading ice hockey
teams in Denmark.

In Sweden and Finland, where ice hockey is more common,
conditions have been critical for growth. The game was first played
in Sweden shortly after the First World War. In 1939 Stockholm
Stadion's artificial ice rink was built. After the Second World War
an indoor facility was built. Ice hockey quickly became the most
popular winter sport in Sweden. In city and town the story was the
same. The early construction of an ice hockey hall in the small town
of Leksand (a municipality in central Sweden of some 15,000 inhabitants), together with enthusiastic local support, has contributed
to the consistent success of the ice hockey club (Aldskogius 1993),
although lit occupies a rather special place in Swedish ice hockey,
as a David among the Goliaths (Aldskogius 1995). The strong local
support is not least due to the ice stadium's function as a spatial link
between club and municipality.

Brynäs, from Gävle, is another well-known ice hockey club in
Sweden which owes much to the spatial conditions. This club's
success in the sixties was attributed to the location of an ice hockey
rink near a heavily populated working-class part of the town with a
large young population. Close contact between players and supporters before, during and after the matches developed (Karlsson 1993),
and Brynäs became the symbol of a successful proletariat in the
Swedish social democratic "Folkhem-state" (Erstrand 1995). Since
post-industrial commercialism in the 1990s, Brynäs was for a period
eliminated from the top ice hockey division. A working-class image
was not a marketable commodity in the new yuppie-Sweden.

Helsinki has two ice hockey worlds. The oldest is the HIFK club
with a Swedish name. It is considered the finest. The other is the
Jokerit club. In the 1960s and 1970s it became the favourite club for
many first generation migrants who flooded into Helsinki from the
provinces during these decades. In their efforts to find a new identity they flocked to support the Jokerit and got their own point of
identification when the new, well-built, Jäähalli was inaugurated in
1966. The club was well marketed by a self-made man, the renowned
"Hjallis" Harkimo. As the Finnish historian Seppo Aalto has written

in his book about Jokerit: "rural Finland changed suddenly into an urban Finland" (Aalto 1992: 18).

The history of Jokerit demonstrates that there is often a close connection between experience, premises and sports. Even if the space for sports has become mono-functional and standardized, loyalty in the form of an intimate sense of togetherness, of place, sportsmen and facilities, is still possible (Bale 1993: 55). Despite norms of standardization and tendencies to *homotopia* (constrained space) in sports, loyalty to a team is still possible in Leksand, Gävle and Helsinki. It is one of the paradoxes in the post-war history of spaces for sport, that sports *homotopia* could be flanked by a corresponding *topophilia*, (love for the place).

Conclusion

The evolution of sports space from the pre-modern to the modern period may be divided into five overlapping stages. This development reveals a trend towards less multi-functional sport spaces and a movement from natural landscape to constructed sports landscape. Modernity has both created a sharp dividing line between spectators and performers, and required a fierce struggle to obtain mono-functional sport spaces.

Mono-functionalism immediately after the Second World War and in the 1960s in particular, resulted in the increasing concentration of sports in urban space. Sometimes this provoked popular opposition.

But, on the other hand, the provision of mono-functional sport space and the separation of the public and the performer have not prevented spectator idealism and strong commitment to the clubs and the sport space. A deeply felt sense of place is still connected with many stadiums and grounds as affective ties with the material and mental environment. The trend towards standardized spaces for sports has not prevented a marked local patriotism and "local sensation" in relation to these spaces, as can be seen – not least – in the ice hockey culture of Leksand and Brynäs in Sweden.

Secondly, it is obvious that the creation of space for sports throughout the Nordic countries – typical for the democratic social-liberal form of societies – has been about cooperation between the private associations, on the one hand, and the state and municipality on the other, but it is also evident that the public authorities have not been equally willing to support the construction of sports facilities everywhere. Here different kinds of political and administrative traditions from country to country have had an effect: it seems that the municipalities in Sweden and Finland have been less reluctant to support spaces for sport than in Denmark where, generally, such steps were not taken until the post-war period.

Thirdly, it is remarkable that the spatial dimension of sports facilities has had a strong impact on the development of sport. Easy access to small handball courts in the Danish countryside, for example, facilitated the spread of handball in rural areas in the 1930s. The peculiarities of sports facilities have also influenced the performance style of clubs, as can be seen from the various ways of playing badminton.

So, as a conclusion, it can be maintained that the question of space and sports facilities during the past 200 years has played a crucial role in the sports history of the Nordic countries. On the other hand, it must also be maintained that research in this field is only at a beginning. There are, as this survey demonstrates, numerous topics to be dealt with for many years to come.

LUTHERANS, CONFORMISTS, SOCIAL DEMOCRATS – AND ATHLETES

Ever since the Second World War historians have been discussing what constituted the European shift from feudalism to capitalism, also called the shift from subject to citizen: in other words the question of modernity. In extension of this, recognizing that this shift in general has been marked by nationalism, they have also discussed the concept of "folk" and "people" which can be seen as synonymous with the concept of "nation". Here, one position claims that the histories of "peoples" are all unique, and all raise their own questions. In contrast to this standpoint is another, the universalistic: that we deny the concept and idea of a people, and instead concentrate on humanity and human rights. This last position is usually assumed by well-meaning humanists and adherents of left-wing politics.

Between these two extremes, there is a middle way, where statements are less categorical and abstract, and more historic. This is found, among other things, in viewing the question in the form of characteristic traits in larger entities, e.g. in a European context. This is the position taken in this article, where the focus is on a Scandinavian context.

Universalism or particularism

Here, the standardized viewpoint is that there is a classic European highway to reason and civilization, namely that which arose when the critical intelligentsia in France and England, provoked by absolutism, set forth a series of educational ideas. From above, these ideas spread via upbringing and education to the idea-arsenal of other classes of society and gave rise to the French revolution with its vision of freedom, brotherhood and equality. With variations, this was to gain universal validity in Western Europe (Toulmin 1995), among other things because it was linked to nationalism; more precisely, the type of nationalism called "political nationalism".

This conception has in turn called forth a response that points out in a homogeneous manner the problematic regarding European history in the 17- and 1800s. It is contended that since 1800 the

LUTHERANS, CONFORMISTS, SOCIAL DEMOCRATS ...   155

histories of Germany and Eastern Europe bear witness to other historical courses of development than that sketched in the above. Not least in a nationalistic respect, where this part of Europe has instead aimed at a cultural nationalism adhering to particularistic rather than universalistic principles. The starting point for this was Herder's incomparable discovery in 1774 of the concept of "a people", which he uses synonymously with "nation". The main idea is that language, culture and mentality form the nucleus of an objective nationalism that exists as a given, and can be rediscovered in the form of a national revival. Today, we would probably say national reflexiveness. This stands in contrast to the subjective nationalism of Western Europe, where, rationally, nationality is a matter of choice (Hettne, Sörlin and Østergård 1998: 79 ff.).

In the German-Roman and Habsburgian world, the concept "Der deutsche Sonderweg" was used as the designation for a particular aspect of this other tradition in Europe. Basically, it is dominated by an anti-nationalistic tendency, which was first expressed in the soulful romanticism, with its feeling for the irrational and that which was not based on reason. A radical revolt against the bright light of rationality arose, and instead, the phenomenon of *Dämmerung* (Sørensen and Stråth 1997. 3) was acclaimed as the designation for a nostalgic longing for holistic communities, where it was not unlimited liberty, but controlled equality in the form of *communitas* ruled. As said of Germany in the 1800s, nowhere in Western Europe was the populace regarded to such a degree as "subjects" and not fellow-citizens. Particularism, not universalism, ruled in Germany, insofar as the organization of society continued to be rooted in a feudal class-society. In Germany, it was not the universalistic *liberté, egalité, fraternité* of civilization that was highly valued, but the ability of the state to shape "machtgeschützte Innerlichkeit", i.e. the individual's heartfelt search for the realization of his innermost potential (Berger, Donovan and Passmore 1999).

A prerequisite for this particularism was that Germany was a "conglomerate-nation". This expression, launched by Swedish historian Harald Gustafsson, refers to the fact that most European states, up through the 16-and 1700s consisted of *Herrschaften* and *Landschaften* with varying legislative, administrative and cultural peculiarities. This was most obviously the case in the German-speaking "nation", but the particularistic tendency was (cf. the following) also prevalent in the Scandinavian countries (Gustafsson 1998).

While the most important political actor of the French enlightenment tradition was the *citoyen*, with universal voting rights and the rights of fellow-citizens, the German tradition was incarnated in the phenomenon of *Bürger*, who to a much greater degree stood for particularism and local interests (Stråth 1992: 113).

The Nordic third way

Scandinavian historic circles have in later years begun to be interested in a third path: Scandinavian political culture, with its ancestors in absolute monarchy and the Swedish "empire". This type of research has gained a steadily stronger position among both Swedish and Finnish historians up through the 1990s, among other things thematized in the anthology The *Cultural Construction of Norden* (Sørensen and Stråth 1997), where the various contributions each show a facet of this Scandinavian Sonderweg.

It is characteristic of the isolation of the Scandinavian Sonderweg that, to a great degree, it has been a question of relations between the culture of a local society with concrete actors, and the goals of the state/central government. In that connection, investigations of historic channels and arenas of dissemination between the local perspective and the perspective of central powers all the way back to the 16-and 1700s has played a major role. From this we can see that the state, in this regard, has had both a hierarchy- and a community-shaping function, with pressure from above and opposition from below in the shape of several disseminatory organs (Gustafsson 1994).

One significant disseminatory function belonged to the local clergy, who played an important role in Scandinavian local societies in the 16-and 1700s, and until the middle of the 1800s, as a mass-communication and administrative link between the state and citizens. The clergy took care of a large number of practical tasks: from population statistics, the notifying of runaway pigs and criminals, to the distribution of grain as assistance in areas hit by crop failure (Gustafsson 2000). In addition to local clergy, another significant disseminatory organ between the state and local society was the so-called "sockenstämmor" (parish assembly) which – as a secular administrative organ – acted as a filter between local society and governmental powers in the construction of a municipal social-assistance state (Österberg 1987, Furuhagen 1991, Jansson 2000). They strengthened their administrative influence in the course of the first decades of the 1600s, and went through a real phase of expansion in the 1700s. That meant that Sweden was one of the best organized and most thoroughly administered nations in Europe (Söderberg 1992: 20). Eva Österberg thinks that in this closely administered society the rural population was given the opportunity of making its voice heard in the political arenas, so that it was possible to obtain influence on the political processes inside the framework of the political system. In opposition to this idea is that of Bengt Sandin, who thinks that local government was never anything but an auxiliary arm of central government (Sandin 1986: 63 f.). This view has, however, been toned down by Peter Aronsson. In the case of Småland, he has shown that the affluent farmers in "sockenstämmor" and "sexmannaråd" (parish assemblies and six men-representatives) had a forum in which they could practice politics in an increasing number of secular areas (Aronsson 1992).

These local administrations formed, along with non-Conformist organizations, the background for the development of Swedish civic society, which in the course of the 1800s found expression in the formation of associations and voluntary organizations such as temperance associations, medical insurance programmes and labour unions (Lindroth 1994). The increasing individualization and demands for personal freedom and independence which also reached Scandinavia in the course of the 17-and 1800s, were supplemented by egalitarian associations as a counterbalance to the tendency to dissociation.

This process took place in all the Scandinavian countries in the course of the 1800s – although with considerable variation. Regardless of whether one fastens upon a relative municipal stagnation, which is strongest in Sweden, and a municipal mobilization, which is strongest in Norway (Jansson 1997), or whether popular enlightenment takes place from above as in Finland or from below as in Norway, and to a certain degree Denmark, (Stenius 1997b), central to this process is a balancing of the relationship between freedom and equality. This, along with the pragmatic construction of enlightenment in Scandinavia, is the main characteristic of Scandinavian "Sonderweg". The citizens of this Sonderweg distinguish themselves as a concept from both citoyen and Bürger by defending both a universalistic individuality of equality and particularistic special interests. The citizen himself (in the 1800s, it was mostly a male-project) emphasized the rights of the individual and Protestant duties, but also holistic collectivism – joining others in associations and mass-organizations. In this, the responsibility of the individual call was coupled with the joint conducting of the tasks at hand.

Occasionally the project was summed up with the aid of a differentiation between three types of citizenship: On the one hand, "state-citizenship", where the state, as in the case of Bismarck, rudimentarily took care of its own, or as in Communist countries, where the state decided what could responsibly be expended on the care and nurture of the individual. On the other hand, "part-citizenship", where the individual has a legitimate right to primarily take care of and pursue his own interests. And then there is "state fellow-citizenship", where the individual is regarded as partly a state-citizen but also as a citizen who allows his interests to be taken care of by a multiplicity of organizations, associations and societies. The individual's interests are taken care of, partly by the state, and partly channelled through voluntary confederations. This latter type of citizenship is characteristic of the Scandinavian model in general – with the variations usually valid for the respective Scandinavian national states (Knudsen 1994). This doubleness – along with the comprehensive civic organization in associations – means that the Scandinavian people belong to the most thoroughly organized in the world, and are in themselves contributors to the conformity which is a Scandinavian peculiarity. The system of popular associations has also, for good or for bad, been a contributor to this conformity.

Associations and popular enlightenment

Associations are characterized by maintaining the individual's right to be an individual: membership of an association is voluntary and personal, and one participates in the activities of the association without any consideration to stand, profession or confession. The organization principle is precisely a measured relation between freedom and equality (Stenius 1987: 43). Here one meets in the middle. In grass-root organizations with individual membership, for example, people adapt to one another and therefore establish a characteristic conformity. A conformity which at first glance is not unlike the universality that marks the standardized classic Western European transition to modernity, but which nevertheless radically distinguishes itself from it by not being a matter of principle, but rather practical and concrete. This means that only with the greatest reluctance is responsibility left to partial cultures and special interests; instead, the principle that the consensus of conversation, discussion and dialogue is to be allowed to penetrate the pores of society is adhered to, and stamped as it were by the universal commonsense of everyday life (Stenius 1997a: 85). The governing of society is to take place like an annual meeting, where everyone has the right to speak, if only one is reasonable, pragmatic and wants what is best for all. As has already been stated, it is not only the principle of voluntariness, but also agreement that marks the Scandinavian type of association (Goldschmidt Salomon 1992).

In the Scandinavian countries this homogenization is rooted in the efforts toward Lutheran-Evangelical propaganda that saw the light of day as early as the 16-and 1700s in the pre-national territorial states' epoch, and which in the Lutheran sphere contributed to the laying of a universalistic-Christian foundation in the public consciousness. Christian universalism was earlier abroad than the political and legal defence of human rights and natural rights. But in the course of the 1800s, when school education was systemized in the shape of governmental school systems, this homogenization and universalization was further strengthened by virtue of nationalism's necessarily inclusive view of fellow citizens, where everyone in the nation was in principle alike and equal national citizens (Hettne, Sörlin and Østergård 1998: 132 ff.). Literacy and military service forcefully strengthened the Scandinavian tendency to conformity.

The literary societies, free churches, pastoral councils, etc. dominated by non-Conformist and Grundvigian thought, probably lie in continuation of the Western European universalistic enlightenment project, and can be seen as its consummation (Kayser Nielsen 1993). But as Øystein Sørensen and Bo Stråth have expressed it, these organizations always have had a slight odour of the barnyard, in the sense that it is not so much the idealistic, utopian stamp that dominates, rather the pragmatic, cunning considerations that rule. Scandinavian enlightenment rationalism is a rationalism of horse-trading. The particularistic side of the matter has constantly played a definitive role. It was not without reason that Folk High School principal Ludvig Schrøder, from the Askov Folk High School – who at any time could be depended on for an idealistic lecture – wanted a barrel of liquid-manure as a present on the occasion of his silver wedding!

It can thus hardly be doubted that what we have here is a special Nordic Sonderweg, with three essential characteristics: a balance between freedom and equality, pragmatism as an organisational principle, and conformity as an organisational form, but there is a one more facet –alongside Christianity, school and conscription – which belongs in this picture.

The contribution of sport to the Nordic third way

It seems strange that the role played by sport and physical education in the development of the distinctive political culture and cultural politics of the Nordic countries has been largely overlooked. In general Nordic education and self-education were from the start tied to sport and organised physical activity (Kayser Nielsen 2003). Precisely because sport – in principle if not in practice – is based on the possibility of being the best on equal terms, it has been tied to the balancing of freedom and equality that seems to be so typically Nordic that one can rightly speak of a special Nordic way. The idea that it is not just consciousness but also the body that should be qualified and developed – and that physical activities contributed decisively to the modernisation of Nordic societies – is characteristic of Norden (Kayser Nielsen 1999).

Physical exercises also have a pragmatic aim: from the beginning there was talk of a combination of educational idealism and matter-of-fact useful aims when the Reventlow brothers introduced physical exercises for the children of farmers on their respective estates. Physical qualifications were the precondition for "industrious" farmers, who, as enterprising citizens, could manage every single pound for the best of the community. One should learn to be civilised in a physical sense also. Soil, consciousness and body should be cultivated.

At the same time, sport is characterised by a certain "democratic" physical conformity: stomachs growl regardless of the social class to which people belong, and at physical competitions the prerequisites of farmers and workers are just as good as those of the middle classes. Just like the Grundtvigians in Denmark, at the beginning of the twentieth century the most visionary labour leaders in all the Nordic countries realised that sport could become an excellent means of demonstrating what the lower classes could achieve when it was not birthright, intellect and education that constituted the authoritative basis. The democratic legitimacy of the body is an essential part of the Nordic Sonderweg.

But the body is not only a maker of equality, it is also a maker of society. By virtue of the incompleteness of our body (we do not have eyes in back of our head, we are not as strong as horses, we cannot kiss ourselves, and so on), we are dependent upon each other. The reciprocity with which we rectify our respective physical lacks therefore demands the inviolability of the Other's body: that we respect the other because we must – and take pleasure in it. Using a concept borrowed from the Durkheimian tradition, one could call it an organic solidarity, in contrast to a mechanical solidarity which is determined by fundamental equality rather than by pragmatic cooperation as in organic solidarity (Kayser Nielsen 1998).

This organic solidarity is not the result of good will or of a contract between people who otherwise pursue their own private interests, such as parts of liberal philosophy view sociality. It is founded in the condition that we are at one and the same time physically final and incomplete and thus both relatively impotent and relatively omnipotent. In our limitation we are dependent on each other. We are abandoned to the condition that we are dependent upon each other.

This may be where one finds the reason for the strong Grundtvigian tradition of letting physical activities (sport, folk dancing, gymnastics exhibitions) be part of general education. These physical activities have had the ability to create communities to an extent that other kinds of general education do not immediately have, creating the possibility of letting the participants not only feel integrated, but also feel like co-creators. The integration takes place in the very act that one helps create. It is something quite different from general education "from above". Songs, parades, folk dancing, and gymnastics carry meaning and create subjectivity themselves – regardless of how rigid and commando-like their elaboration may have been. Again: it is a question of letting the subject realise his inner potentials – in the framework of the conformity and consensus of the community – not of obstinately insisting on one's own individual rights.

Conformity and its roots

A number of researchers have attempted to investigate the roots of Scandinavian conformity. In that connection, Lars Bergquist has emphasized frugality and simplicity as counterbalance to "Italian" mores and customs, and makes himself spokesman for the view that Scandinavian national fellow-citizens take pride in behaving with a suitable mix of informality, group solidarity and social equality with distrust of hierarchies and social ladders (Bergquist 1997). In his turn, Henrik Stenius has fastened on the Scandinavian ideal of conformity, as well as the Scandinavian work ethic: For reasons of self-discipline and the benefit of society, both orthodoxy and Pietism demanded that everyone should work. Work is seen as the virtuous opposite of laziness and as an effective means of protection against the temptations of the flesh (Stenius 1997a and 1997b). Nina Witocheck has emphasized the interaction between Christian, bourgeois virtues, pastoral patriotism and individualism as being the most important foundation of the Scandinavian system of values (Witoszek 1997). According to these researchers, however, the definitive common traits, apart from the work ethic and ideals of freedom, are self-discipline and conformity as well as practical universalism linked to Christianity. Pietism and the religious revivals in Scandinavia in general, and in Norway in particular, easily became part of a nationally coloured process of modernization (Thorkildsen 1998).

Linked to this stress on the Lutheran-Protestant inheritance, Danish historian Claus Bjørn has pointed to the definitive influence of the Reformation on popular enlightenment. According to him there is a fairly straight line from Luther's idea of common priesthood to public libraries. With the implementation of the Reformation, it was necessary to take the populace seriously, regardless of rank, sex, or status. This, however, did not prevent the clergy from being more teachers and educationalists than celebrants. The Protestant church service became a service of the word to a great degree, and in that regard the first versions of Danish and Swedish hymnbooks were also provided with a considerable content of texts, ranging from Bible texts for the liturgical year, the catechism, with explanations, and prayers for family services (Bjørn 1997). The Swedish church law of 1686 and the school ordinance for Denmark and Norway commanded the institution of a public school, and similarly, Swedish clergy were ordered to leave no stone unturned when questioning the parish households, and it was likewise laid down that a well-executed confirmation was an admission ticket for entrance into marriage.

The tendency gained speed with Pietism, Herrnhuterism and the non-Conformist movements, all of which demanded individual literacy. Private philanthropic educational societies like The Danish Agricultural Society of 1769 and, in 1794, the first Sweden-Finland literary society library in Vasa, further spread literacy and enlightenment – later to be embraced by the Folk High Schools and, finally, the working classes. In 1880, MD Anton Nyström established Stockholm's *Arbetarinstitut* (Worker's Institute), which became a model for similar initiatives in other cities in Scandinavia, and in the course of the 19th century, the worker's movement itself took over, with *Arbetarnas Bildningsförbund* in Sweden in 1912, *Arbejdernes Oplysningsforbund* (The Workers Educational Association) in Denmark in 1924 and in Norway in 1931 (Bjørn 1997: 231). These federations have, according to Bjørn, roots not only in the period of Enlightenment, but all the way back to the Lutheran reformation. The Scandinavian worker's movement, seen in this perspective, is a Lutheran-Protestant inheritance.

In this connection, Swedish professor emeritus in Ethics, Ragnar Holte, in an article on Lutheran tradition in a secularized Scandinavia, has pointed out that Luther's quite elitist view of *who* is reasonable, and therefore has the right to speak for others, is democratized by the dissolution of the nobility-ruled state. This does not imply a dissolution of the idea that political life is still to be run by natural

reason, on the contrary, it implies that democratically elected politicians are now seen as being the foremost practitioners of natural
reason; but these are in turn chosen by the populace, who with
their right to vote, likewise make use of their natural reason (Holte
1997: 95). In other words, this implies an idea of a symbiotic fel-
lowship, based on reason, between elected and electors. A symbiosis
that among other things is caused by the Lutheran-coloured public
enlightenment and training in the use of reason.

Religious virtues of frugality could also be flanked by a clear
tradition for demanding one's right in return for doing one's duty,
i.e., to achieve social legitimacy by being diligent and hard-working.
Here, one adapted oneself to paternalistic ethics, which also allowed
one to – diligently – participate in the social benefits with their corresponding demands for a "decent" life-style that were offered in
the course of the 20th century. Asceticism and the work ethic were
supplemented by the possibility of – quite legitimately, since one had
behaved so properly and sensibly – to help oneself to whatever was
on offer. Here Keynesian ideas could easily come to their rightful
place with a Scandinavian Protestant-Pietistic inheritance. In step
with this, Scandinavian democracy developed (cf. below) from a
formal democracy of rights to that of a "gift" democracy, where the
state and its citizens exchanged confidence, care, and loyal behaviour
with one another (Kayser Nielsen 2001).

And so, here we can return to our point of departure. Any discussion on the transition from feudalism to capitalism, as it is called in
Marxist terms, and the transition from subject to citizen – likewise
any discussion of when Modernity takes hold, and of what it consists – cannot escape the historic circumstance that each of these
breakthroughs takes place in the sphere of national states (Hettne,
Sörlin and Østergård 1998: 45 ff.).

This implies that we must take into consideration that there is not
just one transition from traditional to modern. The modern is not
found as abstract modernity, but as historical-concrete constructions
determined by the conditions for the establishment and construction
of national states. The fact is, regardless of whether we are speaking
of old national states like Denmark and Sweden or young national
states like Norway and Finland, that Modernity is historically and
spatially allocated – and coloured by specific circumstances.

A Scandinavian model – or four different ones?

The Scandinavian concept of democracy has undergone a transformation in the course of the past 150 years. From having been conceived as a right, which slowly but surely was won by all adults in all classes of society, democracy changed in the course of the interwar years – partly in resistance to rightist-populism, partly inspired by it – to become a duty. The individual citizen was encouraged to participate in the collective obligation, and to be jointly responsible for the goals being pursued, in return for receiving a selection of universalistic social and cultural benefits, life-historically broadly dispersed. This duty was thus intimately linked to the consuming citizen, who received services and servicing from society in return for backing his/her society up democratically, in both attitude and behaviour. In exchange for loyalty, it became a duty to accept the governmentally organized benefits offered by society with the right mindset and the correct behaviour. This fundamental idea has had its prominent political actors:

Ever since the passing of the "August Law" in Denmark on August 7th, 1914, which was administered by the Social Liberal Party then in power, and ever since the same government in 1917 in a combination of treasury-thinking and the hope of behavioural regulation raised the price of a bottle of snaps from 1½ DKK, to 10 DKK, this party has adhered to the principle of teaching citizens responsible public-mindedness. The Social Democratic Party has instead been the heir to a patriarchal, ethically based solitude for the population, with the state as social patronage. In both cases we find a solicitous and overriding relation to the populace.

In the other Scandinavian countries, the situation looks slightly different. The structure is basically the same, but the balance between the actors is different. In Norway, the popular liberal-democratic wing, among other things, thanks to a clear regional rooting in West Norway, and an equally clear centring on main issues like the language issue and the temperance issue, has been able to maintain a much more independent profile in relation to civil service state than in Denmark. Naturally this is also because the civil service state was to such a degree seen as a Danish inheritance: in spite of the fact that even the Liberal Party took part in this inheritance (Sørensen 1998). A consequence has been that popular democracy has been both strong and oppositional and has been able to defend a radical-democratic tradition alien to the Danish way of thinking (Nerbøvik 1969).

In Sweden the idea is just as alien. Here, one cannot speak of opposition between the State and the Liberals as in Norway and Denmark. The national liberal tradition was present in Sweden, represented by people like Johan Gabriel Richert and Carl Jonas Love Almqvist (Jansson 1990: 346 f.), but it never became as strong as in Norway and Denmark. This meant that the civil service state was not to such a great extent contested from within and attacked from without. The power of government and the legitimacy of the civil service was stronger and lasted longer than in Denmark and especially in Norway. Actually, it continued so long that the Swedish worker's movement had time to lay claim to the "folkrörelses" (popular movement) elements from the 1800s that could also have developed into a new liberal-democratic wing in Sweden. Instead the result was now a large, also personal, coalescence between state, working class and popular movements consummated with "folkhemsforestillingen" (the idea of peoples' home). It was able to mobilize popular efforts, intellectual and liberal civil servants in a cooperative effort where everyone put his hand to the same plough. In 1911 and 1917 no less than two-thirds of the second chamber's members of Parliament (Riksdag) – mainly social Democrats and Liberals – were also members of the temperance movement.

In Finland, the liberal tradition, apart from economic questions, has always been as good as non-existent (Stenius and Turunen 1995). Likewise, a political forum for the discussion of political ideas was lacking, in that the "Landdag" was not assembled from 1809 to 1863. Consequently, it was to be the University, especially the Law Department, that acted as a forum for discussion. The National-Democratic potential was therefore linked to an idea of the constitution, where an elite – to a far greater degree than in the other Scandinavian counties – acted as mediators between state and citizens (Jansson 1997). At the same time, this furthered a legalistic tradition, rather than a popular-dialogic. There was more will to work *for* the people than *through* the people (Alapuro 1994: 68). In Fennoman ("Old Finns") ideology, civic society was closely linked to the state, and the Fennoman Party referred to itself as a state party. This took place as a factor in a distancing from any emphasis on special interests and particularism. Accordingly, there was very little tendency to recognize others' special interests. An attempt to found a Liberal party was thwarted by just one article written by Fennoman and statesman J.V. Snellman. The political possibilities of mobilizing opposition were therefore poorer than in the rest of Norden.

The result was a close cooperation between university educated politicians and the rural population, which in the interwar years was violently threatened by a right-radicalization of certain parts of the rural population, but never completely brought to an end. While the Swedish "folkrörelser" started from below, the comparable Finnish movements were initiated from above under Fennoman – bureaucratic hegemony. It is hardly a coincidence that the Finnish word "kansalainen" means both state citizen and civic citizen. Etymologically, people and state have the same root in the Finnish "kansa" (Pulkkinen 1999: 126 ff.). It is not so markedly bureaucratic in the remaining Scandinavian countries, but Dag Østerberg's old dictum that it is impossible to write the history of Scandinavia without referring to Hegel is still valid. Scandinavia has a peculiar history, in that the state not only cares for "the people" as a particularistic whole, but also for what in the Nordic languages is called "vanligt folk", i.e., the individual citizen with universalistic rights and duties (Engman 2000): Duties to both government and society.

"The great Scandinavian alliance" between state, society and citizens

Thus there are clearly both differences and similarities between the Scandinavian countries' shaping of democracy, in time as well as in space. In general, however, there are two great common denominators (Kettunen 1997).

Firstly, the historic formation of the Scandinavian welfare states rests on a relation to three different contexts: the capitalistic spirit, the socialistic utopia, and the idealized tradition of the independent farmer. The first of these contexts is common to all Western nations, the second is common to those Western countries where the Social Democratic Party is or has been in power, the third is shared only with the remaining Scandinavian countries, insofar as it is only here that the working class and its life situation has been interpreted in the light of an agricultural society, and democratic politics has been arranged so as not to conflict with this.

Secondly – and related – it is clear that the fulcrum for coop-eration between farmers and workers, which is also the point of departure for the Scandinavian welfare model, and a link in the development of rights-democracy to a "duty" and "gift" democracy, rests on a moral foundation. The Red-Earth collaboration in the 1930s, which is the institutional forum for these three elements, was not only about compromises between conflicting parts and special interests, but also about the establishment of what Pauli Kettunen has called "a virtuous circle between economics, politics and ethics" (Kettunen 1997: 158).

The basic idea is, in other words, to establish a moral sense of belonging. Society in the Scandinavian model is a moral relationship more than an organizational form. This is also the case for govern-ment in society, insofar as government also has a moral, more than a technical-administrative, responsibility. It is this peculiarity which is so difficult to understand for non-Scandinavians, and which at the same time hinders the integration of foreigners who have no historic share in the development of democracy from a rights-democracy to a "duty" and "gift" democracy, but must keep to the formal rules of a rights-democracy – and who are therefore regarded by many otherwise democratically-minded people as unsuited to participate in the "great Scandinavia symbiosis".

Conclusion

I began by raising the question of whether the history of the people and the nation was absolutely particularistic – or if one can speak of common characteristics valid for larger entities. In that connection it appears from the above that the people and nations of Scandinavia have a common history on one level of abstraction, but also that they are different and have their own histories, on another level of abstraction.

One important common characteristic is the Lutheran heritage, another is the relatively high legitimacy of the governing power, and its ability to enter into a symbiosis with municipal authorities and the organizations and institutions of civic society. This inheritance is identical with a certain political freedom and equality and has contributed to clearing the path for a "Western" subjective, universalistic political nationalism. This, however, has never been dominant, in that it has constantly been flanked by particularistic considerations of local and regional conditions as well as of pragmatic real-political considerations. The Scandinavian "Sonderweg" is therefore for the most part comprised of a relatively effortless harmonization between state, peoples and population. In Scandinavia more than anywhere else, the elitist, pompous, class-neglecting concept "people" has always been restrained in respect for "the people", in the sense of the population in general.

REFERENCES

Aalto, Seppo 1992: *Jokerit liukkaalla jäällä*. Helsingfors: Team-Erica.

Aggeboe, Kurt and Vig Nielsen 1988: *Horne Idrætsforening 85 år – Horne Idræts-park 50 år*. Varde.

Alapuro, Risto 1994: Nineteenth-Century Nationalism in Finland, in: Øystein Sørensen (ed.): *Nordic Paths to National Identity*. KULTs skriftserie, no. 1. Oslo: The Norwegian Research Council.

Aldskogius, Hans 1993: *Leksand, Leksand, Leksand*. Stockholm: Gidlund.

Aldskogius, Hans and Olof Moen 1994: Idrotten – en folkrörelse i geografisk perspektiv, in: Barbro Blomberg and Sven-Olof Lindquist (eds.): *Den regionala särarten*. Lund: Studentlitteratur.

Alstrup, Aksel 1950: *Jysk Fodbold i Fortid og Nutid*, vol. 1 & 2. Odense: Arncrones forlag.

Aronsson, Peter 1992: *Bönder gör politik. Det lokala självstyret som social arena i tre Smålandssocknar 1680-1850*. Bibliotheca Historica Lundensis 72. Lund: Lund University Press.

Baggesen, Jens 1907: *Udvalgte digtninger*. Copenhagen and Christiania.

Bale, John 1992: *Sport, Space and the City*. London: Routledge.

Bale, John 1996: Homotopia? The Sameness of Sports Places, in: Henning Eichberg and Jørn Hansen (red.): *Bewegungsräume. Körperanthropologische Beiträge*. Butzbach-Griedel: Afra Verlag.

Bayertz, Kurt 1990: Biology and beauty – science and aesthetics in fin de siècle Germany, in: Mikulas Teich and Roy Porter (eds.): *Fin de siècle and its legacy*. Cambridge: Cambridge University Press.

BBU-Bornholms Boldspil Union (ed.) 1957: *Fodbold gennem 50 år*. Rønne.

Berger, Stefan, Mark Donovan and Kevin Passmore 1999: Apologias for the nation-state in Western Europe since 1800, in: Stefan Berger, Mark Donovan and Kevin Passmore (eds.): *Writing National Histories. Western Europe since 1800*. London and New York: Routledge.

Berggren, Henrik 1995: *Seklets ungdom. Retorik, politik och modernitet 1900-1939*. Stockholm: Tiden.

Berggren, Henrik 1997: Modernity and the Nordic Concept of Youth, in: Øystein Sørensen and Bo Stråth (eds.): *The Cultural Construction of Norden*. Oslo: Scandinavian University Press 1997.

Bergquist, Lars 1997: Nordisk värdegemenskap. Tanke och språk, in: Göran Bexell and Henrik Stenius (eds.): *Värdetraditioner i nordiskt perspektiv*. Lund: Lund University Press.

Björkman, Ingmar 1987: *Svenska Finlands Idrottsförbund 1912-1987*. Helsingfors: SFI

Björkman, Ingmar 1997: *Idrottsföreningen Kamraterna r.f. 100 år för Finlands Idrott*. Helsinki: Kamraten, vol. 71, no. 2.

Bjørn, Claus 1997: Det oplyste folk, in: Henrik S. Nissen (ed.): *Nordens historie 1397-1997*. 10 essays. Copenhagen: DRMultimedie.

Boisen, P.O. 1800: *Betragtninger over vigtige Optrin i det huslige Liv*. Copenhagen.

Bruhn, Verner 1979: *Plint og talerstol. Træk af gymnastik- og ungdomsforeningernes historie i Ribe Amt*. Agerbæk: RAGU.

Brummer, Hans Henrik 1995: *Anders Zorn. Til øjets fryd og fædrelandets forher-ligelse*. Copenhagen: Fogtdals forlag. Kunstklubben.

Bunkeflod, H.C. 1786: *Forsøg til viser for Spindeskolerne*. Copenhagen.

Buurgaard, Lise 1997: *J.F. Willumsen: Bjerget, kvinden, selvet*. Esbjerg.

Böling, Rainer et al. 1986: *Närpes Hembygdsbok*. Närpes: Närpes hembygs-förenings förlag.

Cederquist, Jonas 1996: Rekordtänkandet i tidig svensk idrottsrörelse, in: *Idrott, historia och samhälle*. *SVIF-nytt* no. 4. Stockholm: Svenska idrottshistoriska föreningen.

Christensen, Olav 1993: *Skiidrett før Sondre. Vinterveien til et nasjonalt selvbilde*. Oslo: Ad Notam Gyldendal.

Cornell, Henrik 1959: *Den svenska konstens historia: Från nyantiken till Konst-närsförbundet*. Stockholm.

Danmarks Statistik (ed.) 1944: *Statistiske Efterretninger*, vol. 30.

Dansk Idræt, various.

Dansk Idræts Forbund (ed.): *Årbog* 1922 (1923).

Dansk Idræts-Forbund (ed.) 1944: *Officielle Meddelelser*, vol. 22, no. 6. Copenhagen.

Dansk Ungdom, various.

Dragehjelm, Hans 1933: Den første legeplads i Danmark, in: *Gymnastisk Tidsskrift 1933*.

Duke, Vic and Liz Crolley 1996: *Football, Nationality and the State*. London: Longman.

Eggum, Arne 1983: *Edvard Munch: Malerier – skisser og studier*. Copenhagen.

Eisenberg, Christiane 1996: Charismatic National Leader: Turnvater Jahn, in: *The International Journal of the History of Sport*, vol. 13, no. 1 – *Special issue: European Heroes*.

Eklund, Artur 1917: *Idrottens filosofi*. Helsinki: Söderström (1970).

Ekstrand, Lars 1995: Brynäs IF och det efterindustriella Gävle, in: Håkan Attius etc: *Den samtida historien. Studier till Gävles 550-årsjubilem 1996*. Stockholm: Carlsson.

Ellenius, Allan 1996: *Bruno Liljefors: Naturen som livsrum*. Stockholm.

Engman, Max 2000: Folket – en inledning, in: Derek Fewster (ed.): *Folket. Studier i olika vetenskapers syn på begreppet folk*. Helsingfors: Svenska litteratursällskapet i Finland.

Faxøe, Einar 1934: Athletik, in: Seier Larsen (ed.): *Idrætten*. Copenhagen: Hjemmets bibliotek

Finell, Helge 1995: *By i förvandling*. Närpes: Närpes hembygdförenings bokförlag.

Finne, Jarl 1937: *Wasa Idrottssällskap 1907-1937*. Vasa: WIS.

Finsk Idrottsblad 1904.

Franzén, Helmer 1993: Med 3 MGK/IR 61 i forsättningskriget 1941-1944, in: Bjarne Smeds (ed.): *Vi ser deras möda*. Övermark Hembygdsförening.

Frosterus, Sigurd 1915: *Olika skönhetsvärden*. Stockholm and Borgå: Bonniers and Schildts förlag.

Frosterus, Sigurd 1946: *Nordiskt i dur och moll*. Helsinki, 1946.

Frykman, Jonas 1992: In Motion. Body and Modernity in Sweden between the World Wars, *Ethnologia Scandinavica 1992*.

Frykman, Jonas 1993a: Becoming the Perfect Swede: Modernity, Body Politics, and National Processes in Twentieth-Century Sweden, in: *Ethnos*,
vol. 58, nos. 3-4.

Frykman, Jonas 1993b: Nationella ord och handlingar, in: Billy Ehn, Jonas
Frykman and Orvar Löfgren (eds.): *Försvenskningen av Sverige. Det na-
tionellas förvandlingar*. Stockholm: Natur och Kultur.

Furuhagen, Björn 1991: Sockenstämmornas sociala kontrol – exemplet Harg
1742-1773, in: *Historisk Tidsskrift*, Sverige 1991, nr. 1.

Garde, Axel 1989: Johannes V. Jensen, en moderne lyriker, in: Bo Elbrønd
Bek and Aage Jørgensen (eds.): *Jordens elsker. Synspunkter på Johannes V.
Jensen*. Copenhagen: Akademisk forlag.

Gaunt, David 1983: *Familieliv i Norden*. Stockholm: Gidlund.

Gillis, John 1974: *Youth and History. Tradition and Change in European Age Relations 1770-Present*. London.

Gjøde Nielsen, Henrik 1994: *Sportens spor. Gymnastik- og idrætshistorie fra Viborg
Amt*. Gymnastik- og Idrætshistorisk Samling, Viborg 1994.

Goksøyr, Matti 1990: Kun et spørsmål om å konkurrere?, in: Else Trangbæk
(ed.): *Den engelske sports gennembrud i Norden*. København.

Goldschmidt Salomon, Karen Lisa 1992: I grunden er vi enige. En ekskursion
i skandinavisk foreningsliv, in: *Antropologi* 25 (1992).

Grinderslev, Niels 1998: Ishockey i Esbjerg i 1940'erne og 1950'erne, in: *Fra
Ribe Amt* 1998.

Grundtvig, N.F.S. 1832: Prolog til Nordens Mythologi eller Sindbilled-Sprog,
in: Kaj Thaning (ed.): *N.F.S. Grundtvig – Skrifter i udvalg*. Copenhagen:
Gyldendal 1965.

Grønfeldt, Harald 1909: Løb, Spring, Kast m. m., in: A.C. Meyer (ed.):
Idrætsbogen, vol. 2. Copenhagen: Chr. Erichsens forlag.

Gustafsson, Harald 1994: Vad var staten? Den tidigmoderna svenska staten:
sex synpunkter och en model, in: *Historisk Tidsskrift – Sverige* 1994, nr. 2.

Gustafsson, Harald 1998: The Conglomerate State: A Perspective on State
Formation in Early Modern Europe, in: *Scandinavian Journal of History*
1998.

Gustafsson, Harald 2000: Præsten som velfærdsforvalter i tidligt moderne
tid, in: Tim Knudsen (ed.)*: Den nordiske protestantisme og velfærdsstaten*.
Aarhus: Aarhus University Press.

Hagman, Kaj 1985: Fotbollens första framsteg, in: IFK Vasa (ed.) *Jubiläumsboken*. Vasa.

Haldin, Valle 1985: IFK:are i IR 61 1941-1944, in: IFK Vasa (ed.) *Jubiläumsboken*. Vasa.

Hallands Idrottsförbund (ed.) 1993: *Hallands idrottshistoria. Et hopp från dåtid
till nutid*. Örkelljunga: Settern.

Hansen, Jørn 1990: Sport and dansk idræt, in: Jørn Hansen and Niels Kayser
Nielsen (ed.): *Idrætshistorisk Årbog* 1990 – regionalt, nationalt og interna-
tionalt.

Hansen, Jørn 1995: Sports- og idrætsfester, in: Else Trangbæk, Jørn Hansen
and Niels Kayser Nielsen (eds.): *Dansk idrætsliv vol. 1: Den moderne idræts
gennembrud 1860-1940*. Copenhagen: Gyldendal.

Hentilä, Seppo 1982: *Suomen työläisurheilun historia* I, *Työväen Urheiluliitto*
1919-1944. Hämeenlinna.

Hettne, Björn, Sverker Sörlin & Uffe Østergård 1998: *Den globala nationalismen. Nationalstatens historia och framtid.* Stockholm: SNS Förlag.

Hjort, V.K. 1799: *Sange for Unge Piger, især med Hensyn til offentlige Arbejdsskoler.* Copenhagen.

Hodne, Ørnulf 1995: *Idrett og fritid. En mellomkrigsstudie i norsk idrettskultur.* Oslo: Novus.

Holgaard Rasmussen, C. 1979: Vesterborg Seminarium, in: *Lolland-Falsters Historiske Samfunds Årbog 1979.*

Holmgaard, Jens 1986: Eksercitsen bag kirken efter gudstjenesten. Var landmilitsen i stavnsbåndstiden en ringe byrde? *Bol og By 1986,* no. 1.

Holte, Ragnar 1997: Luthersk tradition i ett sekulariserat Norden, in: Göran Bexell and Henrik Stenius (eds.): *Värdetraditioner i nordiskt perspektiv.* Lund: Lund University Press.

Horsens Avis 13. 1. 1947.

Hulden, Lars 1980: Lokalspråk och romanprosa, in: Yrjö Varpio (ed.): *Bilden av ett folk: En festskrift ill Väinö Linna.* Helsinki: Schildts.

Högnäs, Sten 1995: *Kustens och skogarnas folk – Om synen på svenskt och finskt lynne.* Stockholm: Atlantis.

Højrup, Ole 1972: Nogle idrætslege i det gamle landsbysamfund, in: Henning Nielsen (ed.): *For sportens skyld.* København: Nationalmuseet.

Højskolebladet 1894, no. 48.

Høybye-Nielsen, Ernst 1969: Den indbyrdes undervisning i den sjællandske almueskole., in: *Årbog for Dansk Skolehistorie 1969.*

Idrottsföreningen Kamraterna (ed.) 1985: *Idrottsföreningen Kamraterne i Sverige under 100 år 1895-1995.* Strängnäs: IFK.

J.C. 1896a: Ere vi svagere end vore Forfædre, in: *Dansk Sundhedstidende* 1896 no. 2.

J.C. 1896b: Sporvogne og Smitte, in: *Dansk Sundhedstidende* 1896 nr. 18.

Jansson, Kjell and Mats Segerblom 1991: *Ryavallen 50 år.* Borås Norma.

Jansson, Torkel 1997: Nationella, regionala och lokala aspekter på nationsbygget i Norden, in: Maria Fremer, Pirkko Lilius and Mirja Saari (eds.): *Norden i Europa. Brott eller kontinuitet?* Helsingfors: Inst. för nordiska språk och nordisk litteratur.

Jansson, Torkel 2000: Två stater – en kultur. Sverige och Finland efter 1809, in: *Historisk Tidskrift* – Sverige 2000: 4.

Janzon, Bode 1992: En hela folkets sak?. Idrottsrörelse och samhällsintressen under 1900-talets första hälft, några hållpunkter, in: *Idrott, historia och samhälle. Svenska idrottshistoriska föreningens årsskrift 1992.*

Jensen, C. Gotlieb 1968: *Vejle Amts Skytte-, Gymnastik- og Idrætsforening 1868-1968.* Vejle.

Jensen, Gotlieb 1981: *Idrætsgruppens 50 års jubilæumsskrift.*

Jensen, Johannes V. 1898: *Einar Elkær.* Copenhagen.

Jensen, Johannes V. 1901. *Mit Forår.* Copenhagen 27. 5. 1901.

Jensen, Johannes V. 1907: *Den ny Verden.* Copenhagen.

Jensen, Johannes V. 1915: *Introduktion til vor Tidsalder.* Copenhagen.

Jensen, Johannes V. 1954: *Digte.* Copenhagen: Gyldendal.

Jensen, Johannes V. 1962: *Aandens spor.* Copenhagen: Gyldendal.

Jensen, Johannes V. 1963: *Kongens fald.* 14. edition. Copenhagen: Gyldendal.

Jensen, Johannes V. 1973: *Mørkets frodighed. Tidlige myter.* Copenhagen: Gyldendal.

Jensen, Johannes V. 1995: *Himmerlandshistorier*. 21. edition. Copenhagen: Gyldendal.

Jussila, Osmo 1999: Finland as a Grand Duchy 1809-1917, in: Osmo Jussila, Seppo Hentilä and Jukka Nevakivi: *From Grand Duchy to a Modern State. A Political History of Finland since 1809*. London: Hurst.

Jørgensen, Frank D. 1999: Kampen om Odense Stadion, in: *Idrætshistorisk årbog 1999*.

Jørgensen, Per 1995a: Dansk Idræts-Forbund dannelse, in: Else Trangbæk, Jørn Hansen and Niels Kayser Nielsen (eds.): *Dansk idrætsliv vol. 1: Den moderne idræts gennembrud 1860-1940*. Copenhagen: Gyldendal.

Jørgensen, Per 1995b: Idrættens struktur, in: Else Trangbæk, Jørn Hansen and Niels Kayser Nielsen (eds.): *Dansk idrætsliv vol. 1: Den moderne idræts gennembrud 1860-1940*. Copenhagen: Gyldendal.

Karlsson, Gunnar 1993: *Brynäs 80 år. Från kvarterslag till mästarklubb*. Malmö Sportförlaget.

Kasvio, Liisa 1992: Den unge samlarens stämningar – värderingar utformas, samlingen blir till, in: Amos Anderssons Konstmuseum (ed.), *Sigurd Frosterus' samling*. Helsinki.

Kayser Nielsen, Niels 1989a: Idræt og offentlig støtte – set i et civilisationsperspektiv, in: *Fortid og Nutid*, vol. 36, no. 3.(1989).

Kayser Nielsen, Niels 1989b: Pengene eller livet – om offentlig støtte til skyttebevægelsen i 1800-tallet, in: *Idrætshistorisk Årbog 1989*. Aabybro.

Kayser Nielsen, Niels 1993/4: Sport und Bauernideologie in der dänischen Sportgeschichte, in: *Stadion. Internationale Zeitschrift für Geschichte des Sports*, vol. 19-20.

Kayser Nielsen, Niels 1993: *Krop og oplysning. Om kropskultur i Danmark 1780-1900*. Odense: Odense Universitetsforlag.

Kayser Nielsen, Niels 1994a: Fra gymnastik til sport, in: *Journalen. Lokal- og kulturhistorisk tidsskrift*, vol. 4, no. 4 (1994).

Kayser Nielsen, Niels 1994b: Hälsa och idrott – en modern och nationell angelägenhet, in: *Idrott, historia och samhälle. Svenska idrottshistoriska föreningens årsskrift 1994*.

Kayser Nielsen, Niels 1994c: Højskole og sport – om idrætten i Vejen, in: *Magasin fra Det kongelige Bibliotek*, vol. 9, no. 2 (1994).

Kayser Nielsen, Niels 1995a: Aktiviteter, in: Else Trangbæk, Jørn Hansen and Niels Kayser Nielsen (ed.): *Dansk idrætsliv*, vol. 1: Den moderne idræts gennembrud 1860-1940. Copenhagen: Gyldendal.

Kayser Nielsen, Niels 1995b: Mellem filantropi og militær – kropskultur og idrætspædagogik i Danmark ca. 1780-1820, *Fund og Forskning i Det kongelige biblioteks Samlinger,* vol. 34. Copenhagen: The Royal Library.

Kayser Nielsen, Niels 1995c: Sport og bondekultur – om foreningsliv i provinsen i mellemkrigstiden, in: *Fortid og Nutid. Tidsskrift for kulturhistorie og lokalhistorie* 1995, no. 1.

Kayser Nielsen, Niels 1995d: The lads from Farre with the red V, in: Anders Linde-Laursen and Jan Olof Nilsson (eds.): *Nordic Landscopes. Cultural Studies of Place*. København og Stockholm 1995.

Kayser Nielsen, Niels 1995e: The Stadium in the City: A Modern Story, in: John Bale and Olof Moen (eds.): *The Stadium and the City*. Keele: Keele University Press.

Kayser Nielsen, Niels 1996: Kropskultur og idrætspædagogik i Danmark ca. 1780-1820, in: *Fund og forskning i Det kongelige Biblioteks samlinger*, vol. 36.

Kayser Nielsen, Niels 1997a: Att tillägna sig det nationella i Norden genom friluftsliv och hälsa – komparativa aspekter, in: Maria Fremer, Pirkko Lilius and Mirja Saari (eds.): *Norden i Europa. Brott eller kontinuitet?* Helsinki: Inst. för nordiska språk och nordisk litteratur.

Kayser Nielsen, Niels 1997b: Håndbold og folkelig idræt i 1930'erne, in: Niels Kayser Nielsen (ed.): *Håndbold i 100 år – et overblik*. Copenhagen: DHF.

Kayser Nielsen, Niels 1997c: "Kritisk loyalitet – om kulturradikalisme i Norden", in: Göran Bexell and Henrik Stenius (eds.): *Värdetraditioner i nordiskt perspektiv: Rapport från ett symposium i Helsingfors*. Lund: Lund University Press, 1997: 173-202.

Kayser Nielsen, Niels 1997d: Movement, Landscape and Sport. Comparative Aspects of Nordic Nationalism between the Wars, in: *Ethnologia Scandinavica 1997*.

Kayser Nielsen, Niels 1997e: Sangleg eller kinddans – træk af debatten om dans i ungdomsforeningerne i mellemkrigstiden, in: *Magasin fra Det kongelige Bibliotek* vol. 12, no. 1 (1997).

Kayser Nielsen, Niels 1998a: Folk, krop og oplysning, in: Jørgen Gleerup and Niels Kayser Nielsen (eds.): *Folkeoplysning, krop og dannelse*. Vejle: DGI.

Kayser Nielsen, Niels 1998b: Ishockey i Horsens – de tabte muligheder, in: *Journalen. Lokal- og kulturhistorisk tidsskrift* 1998, no. 1.

Kayser Nielsen, Niels 1999: Idræt og nationsdannelse i de nordiske lande. Forskelle og fællestræk, in: Bjarne Stoklund (ed.): *Kulturens nationalisering. Et etnologisk perspektiv på det nationale*. København: Museum Tusculanum.

Kayser Nielsen, Niels 2001: *Den selvhjulpne, den modvillige og den forbrugende demokrat – en nordisk historie*. Arbejdspapir, no.10. Department of History, Aarhus University.

Kayser Nielsen, Niels 2003: Kroppens dannelse og dannelsens krop, in: Rune Slagstad, Ove Korsgaard and Lars Løvlie (eds.): *Dannelsens forvandlinger*. Oslo: Pax.

Kern, Stephen 1994: *The Culture of Time and Space 1880-1918*. Cambridge, Mass.: Harvard University Press (1983).

Kettunen, Pauli 1997: The Society of Virtuous Circles, in: Pauli Kettunen and Hanna Eskola (eds.): *Models, Modernity and the Myrdals*. Helsingfors: Renvall-Institute Publications, no. 8.

Klinge, Matti 1988: *Från lojalism till rysshat*. Helsinki: Söderströms.

Knudsen, K. A. 1911: *Øvelseslære. Forklaring af typiske gymnastiske Øvelser,* 5th ed. Copenhagen: J. Frimodt.

Knudsen, Tim 1994: Den svenske model fra ideal til krise, in: *Den jyske Historiker*, no. 68 – Regionen i historien.

Kongsgaard, Herlev et al. (ed.) 1991: *Spjaldhallen gennem 25 år*. Spjald: Spjald Fritidscenter.

Korsgaard, Ove 1982: *Kampen om kroppen. Dansk idræts historie gennem 200 år*. Copenhagen: Gyldendal.

Korsgaard, Ove 1986: *Krop og kultur. Andelsbønernes gymnastik mellem almuens leg og borgerskabets sport*. Odense: Odense Universitetsforlag.

Krogh, L.F.C. 1911: *Skyttesagen i Danmark gennem halvtredsindstyve Aar*. Copenhagen: Overbestyrelsen for de danske Skytteforeninger.

Krogh, Leila 1987: *Løvens breve: J F. Willumsens breve til Alice Krogh 1899-1923*. Frederikssund.

Krogh, Leila 1995: *Fiktion og virkelighed: J F. Willumsens fotografier*. Frederikssund.

Laine, Leena 1992: Urheilu valtaa mielet, in: Teijo Pyykkönen (ed.): *Suomi uskoi urheiluun. Suomen urheilun ja liikunnan historia*. Liikuntatieteellisen Seuran julkaisu, no. 131. Helsinki: VAPK-Kustannus.

Lambek, Claus 1906: *Verdsligt Aandsliv hos Folket*. Copenhagen.

Laugesen, Peter 1992: *Gallén-Kallela*. Copenhagen.

Laurin, Carl G. 1917: *Folklynnen*. Stockholm: Norstedt och söner,

Liedman, Sven-Eric 1997: *Mellan det triviala och det outsägliga: Blad ur humanioras och samhällsvetenskapernas historia*. Göteborg.

Lind, John 1989: Mellem "venska" og "vinska". Finsk. Fra almuesprog til statsbærende kultursprog. Copenhagen: University of Copenhagen: Dept. of Finnish.

Lindberg, Håkan (ed.) 1994: Kampen om Gamla Ullevi, in: Håkan Lindberg (ed.): *Makriller, kval och gröna raketer. GAIS – jubileumsbok 1894-1994*. Göteborg: GAIS.

Lindén, Herbert 1985: IFK-rörelsens uppkomst, in: IFK Vasa (ed.) *Jubiläumsboken*. Vasa.

Lindroth, Bengt 1994: *Sverige och odjuret. En essä om den goda svenska traditionen*. Stockholm: Moderna tider.

Lindroth, Jan 1974: *Idrottens väg till folkrörelse. Studier i svensk idrottsrörelse till 1915*. Uppsala: Studia historica upsaliensia 60.

Lindroth, Jan 1987: *Idrott mellan krigen. Organisationer, ledare och idéer i den svenska idrottsrörelsen 1919-39*. Stockholm: HLS förlag.

Lindroth, Jan 1993: *Gymnastik med lek och idrott*. Stockholm: HLS förlag.

Lindholm, Tor 1995: *Mitt Viborg*. Helsinki: Skrifter utgivna av Svenska Folkskolans vänner, serie III, vol. 10.

Loland, Sigmund 1995: *Idrett, kultur og samfunn*. Oslo.

Lund, Elof 1993: Hisingens försvunna fotbollsplaner – och klubbarna kring dem, in: *Idrottsarvet. Årsbok för Idrottsmuseet i Göteborg 1993*.

Lyngaa, Mogens 1995: Et tilbageblik, in: RAGU (ed.): *Håndboldjubilæum 50 år*.

Löfgren, Orvar 1992: Rum og bevægelse, in: Kirsten Hastrup (ed.): *Den nordiske verden*, bd. 1. København: Gyldendal.

Matsuda, Matt K. 1996: *The Memory of the Modern*. New York and Oxford: Oxford University Press.

Meinander, Henrik 1991: Karaktärsdaning framförallt! En skiss av Carl Svedelius, pedagog och idrottsideolog av nordiska mått, in: *Idrott, historia, samhälle. Svenska idrottshistoriska föreningens årsskrift 1991*.

Meinander, Henrik 1994: *Towards a Bourgeois Manhood. Boys' Physical Education in Nordic Secondary School 1880-1940*. Helsinki: Finnish Society of Science and Letters.

Meinander, Henrik 1996: *Lik martallen som rågfältet. Hundra år finlandssvensk gymnastik*. Helsingfors: FSG.

Mellemgaard, Signe and Niels Kayser Nielsen 1996: Body Culture – Between the International, the National and the Local, in: John T. Lauridsen and Margit Mogensen (eds.): *Copenhagen – the Gateway to Europe*. Copenhagen: The Royal Library, The Danish National Archieves and The Royal Danish Arsenal Museum.

Moen, Olof 1992: *Från bollplan till sportcentrum. Idrottsanläggningar i samhällsbyggande under 100 år*. Stockholm: Byggforskningsrådet.

Moen, Olof 1995: Scales and Values in Stadium Development: A Tale of Two Ullevis, in: John Bale and Olof Moen (eds.): *The Stadium and the City*. Keele: Keele University Press.

Moltesen, Erik 1923: *J.F. Willumsen: Introduktion til hans Kunst*. Copenhagen: Levin and Munksgaard.

Mønster, P.H. 1803: Om Svømme-Øvelser og deres Fremgang hos os som Indbydelse til offentlige Øvelser, hvorved Det gymnastiske Institut høitideligholder sin første Olympiade eller fierde Aarsfest. København. The Royal Danish Library: KB. 17-283 40. Unpublished.

Nachtegall, V.V.F.F. 1820: Brev til Jonas Collinsen. 6.8.1820. The Royal Danish Library, Collinske Brevsamling XXIIIb. Unpublished.

Nachtegall, V.V.F.F. 1828: *Lærebog i Gymnastik*. Copenhagen.

Nachtegall, V.V.F.F. 1831: *Gymnastikkens Fremgang i Danmark fra dens første Indførelse i Aaret 1799 indtil Udgangen af Aaret 1830*. Copenhagen.

Nachtegall, V.V.F.F. 1832. Brev til F.C. Sibbern 5.11.1832. The Royal Danish Library. Add. 1040, 4. Unpublished.

Nachtegall, V.V.F.F. 1840: Kortfattet Fremstilling af min Virksomhed for Gymnastikkens Indførelse og udbredelse fra den første Begyndelse i Aaret 1799 indtil udgangen af Aaret 1840. The Royal Danish Library: KB. NKS 1361-2. Unpublished.

Nerbøvik, Jostein 1969: *Antiparlumentariska straumdrag i Noreg 1905-1914. Ein studie i motvilje*. Oslo: University Press.

Nielsen, Henrik Gjøde 1994: *Sportens spor. Gymnastik- og idrætshistorie fra Viborg Amt*. Viborg: Gymnastik- og idrætshistorisk samling.

Nielsen, Holger 1909: Håndbold, in: A.C. Meyer (ed.): *Idrætsbogen. Populære Vejledninger i Udøvelsen af Gymnastik og dansk Idræt udarbejdede af Fagmænd*, bd. 2. Copenhagen: Chr. Erichsens forlag.

Nitschke, August 1996: *Körper in Bewegung: Gesten, Tänze und Räume im Wandel der Geschichte*. Stuttgart: Kreuz Verlag.

Nyqvist, Nils-Erik 1986: *Sextiettan: Infanteriregimente 61 1941-44*. Vasa: Svensk Österbottniska Samfundet nr. 42.

Nyström, Hilding 1994: *Krigare 1944: Från Svir till Karelska Näset*. Helsinki: Schildts.

Nørr, Erik 1994: *Skolen, præsten og kommunen. Kampen om skolen på landet 1842-1899*. Copenhagen: Jurist- og Økonomforbundets forlag.

Olsson, Daniels Sven 1983: Ett folk som äter träd och dricker vatten, tvingar ej fanan, än mindre någon man – om dalkarlar och idrott i äldre tid, in: Birgitta Dandanell (ed.): *Dalaidrottens historia. Dalarnas Hembygsbok 1983*. Falun: Dalarnas fornminnes och hembygdsförbund.

Olsson, Leif "Loket" 1991: Mässhallen – mitt andra hem, in: *Idrottsarvet. Årsbok för Idrottsmuseet i Göteborg1991*.

Paludan, C. (ed.) 1979: Matthias Lundings rejsedagbog 1787, *Kulturminder*, 3. rk, bd. 2. Copenhagen: Selskabet for dansk kulturhistorie.

Paludan, Jacob s. a.: Især om Tonio Krøger, in: *Tonio Krøger*. Copenhagen.

Pedersen Dømmestrup, A. 1930: Idræt!, in: *Dansk Ungdom og Idræt* 1930, no. 28.

Pedersen, Henning and Peter Kjeldsen 1993: *Store Brønderslev Marked gennem 150 år*. Brønderslev: Lokalhistorisk Arkiv.

Peitersen, Birger 1973: Ludvig Reventlow og almuens undervisning i 1780'erne, in: *Årbog for Skolehistorie*.

Persson, Lennart K. 1994: När gudaborgen föll – om idrottsplatsen Walhallas öde i samband med Göteborgs jubileum 1923, in: *Idrottsarvet. Årsbok för Idrottsmuseet i Göteborg*.

Persson, Lennart K. 1997: Handbollens uppkomst och utveckling – internationella, svenska och göteborgska perspektiv, in: *Idrottsarvet. Årsbok för Idrottsmuseet i Göteborg*.

Persson, Lennart K. and Thomas Pettersson 1995: *Svensk Friidrott 100 år*. Stockholm: Sellin.

Pred, Allan 1995: *Recognizing European modernities. A montage of the present.* London: Routledge.

Pulkkinen, Tuija 1999: One Language, One Mind. The Nationalist Tradition in Finnish Political Culture, in: Tuomas M.S. Lehtonen (ed.): *Europe's Northern Frontier. Perspectives on Finland's Western Identity.* Helsingfors: PS-Kustannus.

Rasch, Aage 1964: *Niels Ryberg. 1725-1804 Fra bondedreng til handelsfyrste.* Aarhus: Universitetsforlaget. Skrifter udgivet af Jysk Selskab for Historie, Sprog og Litteratur 12.

Reventlow, C.B. 1902: *En dansk statsmands hjem omkring aar 1800*, bd. 1. Copenhagen.

Reventlow, J.L. Pro Memoria of 30 Jan. 1794, J. Larsen (ed.) 1900: *Pædagogiske afhandlinger af L. Reventlow. Til opdagelsens historie. Aktstykker til opdragelsens historie* 1, Tillæg 1899-1900. Copenhagen: Vor Ungdom.

Riordan, Jim and Arnd Krüger 1999: Introduction, in: Jim Riordan and Arnd Krüger (eds.): *The International Politics of Sport in the 20th Century.* London and New York: Spon.

Rostrup, H. 1987: *Miranda i Danmark. Francisco de Mirandas danske rejsedagbog 1787-1788.* Copenhagen: Rhodos.

Rydén, Per 1994: *Solskensolympiaden. Essäer.* Stockholm: Ellerström.

Römpötti, Kalevi 1995: Sotilasurheilu suunnan näyttäjänä, in: *Finlands idrottshistoriska förenings Årsbok* 1995.

Samuelsen, Eivind (ed.) 1983: *Idræt i Aalborg gennem 100 år.* Aalborg: Idrætssammanslutningen SIFA.

Samuelsson, Helge 1995: Gamla Ullevi är adressen där fotbollsminnena bor…, in: *Idrottsarvet. Årsbok för Idrottsmuseet i Göteborg* 1995.

Sandin, Bengt 1986: *Hemmet, gatan, fabrikken eller skolan. Folkundervisning och barnuppfostran i svenska städer 1600-1850.* Lund: Arkiv.

Schmidt, Lars-Henrik and Jens Erik Kristensen 1986: *Lys, luft og renlighed. Den moderne socialhygiejnes fødsel.* Copenhagen: Akademisk forlag.

Segerblom, Mats 1986: *Boråsidrotten kring sekelskiftet.* Borås: Norma.

Skjerk, Ole 2001: Dameudvalgets inderlige Overflødighed. Kvindehåndbold i Danmark 1900-1950. Ph.D. dissertation. Institute for Sports. Copenhagen University.

Slagstad, Rune 1998: *De nasjonale strateger.* Oslo: Pax.

Slagstad, Rune 2003: Folkedannelsens forvandlinger, in: Rune Slagstad, Ove Korsgaard og Lars Løvlie (eds.): *Dannelsens forvandlinger*. Oslo: Pax.

Stang, Ragna 1978: *Mennesket og kunstneren Edvard Munch*. Copenhagen.

Stenius, Henrik 1981: Fritidsvecken i Helsingfors på 1870-talet, in: Max Engman etc. (eds.): *My darling Clio. Vänskrift till Jerker A. Eriksson*. Helsingfors.

Stenius, Henrik 1987: *Frivilligt, jämlikt, samfällt. Föreningsväsendets utveckling i Finland fram till 1900-talets början med speciellt hänsyn till massorganisationsprincipens genombrott*. Helsingfors: Svenska litteratursällskapet.

Stenius, Henrik 1992: Finskhetsrörelsens historia fortfarande oskriven, in: *Historisk Tidskrift för Finland*, vol. 77, no. 2

Stenius, Henrik 1993: Den politiska kulturen i Nordens ontologi. Modell eller icke? Vara eller icke vara?, in: Godelieve Laureys, Niels Kayser Nielsen and Johs. Nørregaard Frandsen (eds.) *Skandinaviensbilleder. En antologi fra en europæisk kulturkonference*. Groningen and Gent: TijdSchrift voor Skandinavistiek.

Stenius, Henrik 1997a: Konformitetsideal blev universalitetsideal, in: Göran Bexell and Henrik Stenius (eds.): *Värdetraditioner i nordiskt perspektiv*. Lund: Lund University Press.

Stenius, Henrik 1997b: The Good Life is a Life of Conformity: The Impact of Lutheran Tradition on Nordic Political Culture, in: Øystein Sørensen and Bo Stråth (eds.): *The Cultural Construction of Norden*. Oslo et al: Scandinavian University Press.

Stenius, Henrik and Ilkka Turunen 1995: Finnish Liberalism, in: Ilkka Lakaniemi, Anna Rotkirch and Henrik Stenius (eds.): *Liberalism*. Renvall Institute Publications, no. 7. Helsingfors: University Printing House.

Stråth, Bo 1992: *Folkhemmet mot Europa. Ett historiskt perspektiv på 90-talet*. Stockholm: Tiden.

Söderberg, Johan 1992. Rättsväsendets utbyggnad i Sverige. Lokala konsekvenser och reaktioner 1550-1750, in: Harald Winge (ed.): *Lokalsamfunn og øvrighet i Norden ca. 1550-1750*. Oslo: Norsk lokalhistorisk Institutt.

Sørensen, Poul 1979: Sporten og friluftslivet, in: Knud Moseholm and Aksel Nellemann (eds.): *Kolding i det tyvende århundrede indtil kommunesammenlægningerne i 1970*, vol. 2. Kolding: Kolding Kommune.

Sørensen, Øystein 1998: Elitenes nasjonsbyggingsprojekter 1770-1945, in: Øystein Sørensen (ed.): *Jakten på det norske*. Oslo: Gyldendal Ad Notam.

Sørensen, Øystein and Bo Stråth (eds.) 1997: *The Cultural Construction of Norden*. Oslo et al: Scandinavian University Press.

Sörlin, Sverker 1995: Filolog i sportkostym – rektor Carl Svedelius, in: Ronny Ambjörnsson and Sverker Sörlin (ed.): *Obemärkta. Det dagliga livets idéer*. Stockholm: Carlssons förlag.

Tandefelt, Marika (ed.) 2002: *Viborgs fyra språk under sju sekel*. Helsinki. Schildts.

Thorkildsen, Dag 1998: Vekkelse og modernisering i Norden på 1800-tallet, in: *Historisk Tidsskrift* – Norge, vol. 77.

Toulmin, Stephen 1995: *Kosmopolis. Hur det humanistiske arvet förfuskades*. Stockholm: Ordfront.

Törnquist Plewa, Barbara 1992: *The Wheel of Polish Fortune. Myths in Polish Collective consciousness during the First Years of Solidarity*. Lund: Lund University – Lund Slavonic Monographs 2.

Ungdom og Idræt, various.

Vagten 1899-1900. Edited by L. Mylius-Erichsen. Republished by Hans Reitzels forlag. Copenhagen 1982.

Vasara, Erkki 1992: Sotaa ja urheilua, in: Teijo Pyykkönen (ed.): *Suomi uskoi urheiluun: Suomen urheilun ja liikunnan historia*. Helsinki: VAPK

Vehviläinen, Olli 1976: die Erforschung des zweiten Weltkrieges in Finland, in: Hannes Saarinen (ed.) 1976: *Reports of the Research Project Finland in the Second World War*, vols. 1-2. Helsinki: Helsinki University.

Veitch, Colin 1985: Play up! Play up! and Win the War! Football, the Nation and the First World War 1914-14, in: *Journal of Contemporary History*, vol. 20, no. 3.

Vidler, Anthony 1994: Psychopathologies of Modern Space, in: Michael S. Roth (ed.): *Rediscovering History. Culture, Politics and Psyche*. Stanford: Stanford University Press.

Villaume, Peter 1802: Om Legemets Dannelse med Hensyn til Menneskets Fuldkommenhed og Lyksalighed, eller om den physiske Opdragelse i Særdeleshed, *Revisionsværk, det hele Skole- og Opdragelsesvæsen angaaende*, bd. 8, edited by J.H. Campe. Copenhagen.

Vind, Ole 1999: *Grundtvigs historiefilosofi*. Copenhagen: Gyldendal.

Wahlbeck, Kaj 1994: *Karelen – med kärlek*. Vasa. Oy FRAM ab.

Wahlqvist, Birger 1993: *Vikingarnas lekar. Vikingen som idrottare*. Stockholm: Atlantis.

Werlauf, E.C. 1873/74: Dansk, især kjøbenhavnske Tilstande og Stemninger ved og efter Overgangen til det nittende Aarhundrede. Efterladte Optegnelser, in: *Historisk Tidsskrift* 4. Rk: IV.

Westerlund, Göran 1995: *Tienhaara. Finlands lås*. Helsinki: Söderströms.

Wikman, K. Rob. V. 1963: "Harry Schauman", in: *Österbottnisk Årsbok* 1963. Vasa: Svensk-Österbottniska Samfundet.

Winding, O.S. 1909: Fodbold, in: A.C. Meyer (ed.): *Idrætsbogen. Populære Vejledninger i Udøvelsen af Gymnastik og dansk Idræt udarbejdede af Fagmænd*, bd. 2. Copenhagen.

Ylikangas, Heikki 1995. *Vägen till Tammerfors*. Helsinki: Söderströms.

Ystad, Ottar 1934: Kroppskulturen i Norge, in: *Dansk Idræt* 1934, no. 4.

Zachau, Inge 1998: Eugène Jansson. Den blå stadens målare, in: Liljevalchs Konsthall (ed.): *Eugène Jansson*. Stockholm.

Zahle, Grete 1994: *Himlens spejl*. Copenhagen.

Örsan, Karl 1994: Bruno Liljefors och idrotten, in: *Idrott, historia och samhälle: Svenska idrottshistoriska föreningens årsskrift* 1994.

Østerberg, Dag 1997: Hegels statslære og den norske socialdemokratiske staten, in: Åsmund Birkeland (ed.): *Den moderne staten*. Oslo: Pax.

Österberg, Eva 1987: Svenska lokalsamhällen i förändring ca. 1550-1850, in: *Historisk Tidskrift – Sverige* 1987, no. 1.